The Arabic, Qur'anic and Islamic Paradigm:

Light, Jewels and Pearls

by

Al-Hajj, Dr. Hassan Hasan Sheikh Salime El-Yacoubi
B.A. (Licence en Droit), Law Degree, M.S., Ph.D.

and

Dr. "Amar" Jane Biddle Merritt El-Yacoubi
A.A., B.F.A., Professional Teaching Degree, M.A., Ph.D.

P.O. Box 4094   Boulder, Colorado   80306   U.S.A.

بسم الله الرحمن الرحيم

Kufic

اُدْعُ إِلَى سَبِيلِ رَبِّكَ بِالْحِكْمَةِ وَالْمَوْعِظَةِ الْحَسَنَةِ وَجَادِلْهُم بِالَّتِي هِيَ أَحْسَنُ

Invite others to the way of your Lord with wisdom and gentle admoni-
tion and debate with them in the best possible manner. 19

وَلْتَكُن مِّنكُمْ أُمَّةٌ يَدْعُونَ إِلَى الْخَيْرِ وَيَأْمُرُونَ بِالْمَعْرُوفِ وَيَنْهَوْنَ
عَنِ الْمُنكَرِ وَأُولَٰئِكَ هُمُ الْمُفْلِحُونَ ۞

Let there be from among you a people who call unto Islam, enjoin
the good and forbid the evil and those will be afforded complete success.

إِنَّ أَكْرَمَكُمْ عِندَ اللَّهِ أَتْقَاكُمْ إِنَّ اللَّهَ عَلِيمٌ خَبِيرٌ ۞

Verily, the best among you, in the sight of Allāh, is the most pious;
Allāh is all-knowing and cognisant of your innermost thoughts.

The Arabic, Qur'anic and Islamic Paradigm:
Light, Jewels and Pearls

To True Islam: The Only Way

TABLE OF CONTENTS

إِنَّ الدِّينَ عِندَ اللهِ الْإِسْلَامُ

i

CHAPTER III

CHAPTER IV

CHAPTER V

To True Islam: The Only Way

CHAPTER VI

APPENDIX

Glossary

Please note that the definitions offered below are not necessarily exactly congruent with the Arabic meanings. Our basic assumption is that no translation in any language can be equivalent to the terminology of **ALLAH** (*subhanahu wa ta'ala*). We are only trying to give the reader who is unfamiliar with Arabic the simple idea of a meaning that he or she can understand as a way of transcending previous, illusionary conceptions.

'Abd. Servant or slave. Everyone is, consciously or unconsciously, *'abd* **ALLAH**, the slave of **ALLAH** (*subhanahu wa ta'ala*).

Al-Hamdu Lillah. Praise and thanks be to **ALLAH** (*subhanahu wa ta'ala*).

ALLAH (*subhanahu wa ta'ala*). God, may He be glorified and exalted. He transcends all opposites and limitations.

Al-Ubudiyyah. Slavery and servitude to **ALLAH** (*subhanahu wa ta'ala*).

Ayat. Signs or indicators in the creation, and also verses of the **Generous Qur'an**. Singular form: **ayah**. Everything is an **ayah**.

Din. A "divinely-ordained" Way of life, meaning a *modus operandi* for *modus vivendi*.

Fitrah. The original, intrinsic and pure essence of creatures, including humanity.

v

Furqan. Criterion for the sharp edge of discrepancy. One of the names for the **Generous Qur'an** is **Al-Furqan**.

Hadith. A narration of the spoken words or the actions of the **Prophet Muhammad** (*prayers and peace of* **ALLAH** *be upon him*).

Halal. An adjective meaning permitted by **ALLAH** (*subhanahu wa ta'ala*).

Haram. An adjective meaning prohibited by **ALLAH** (*subhanahu wa ta'ala*).

'Ibara. An allegorical example *par excellence* that is an indicator for understanding a particular meaning or phenomenon. Literally, it implies "to go through" an experience in order to understand the value behind that experience. The individual metamorphoses as a result of this process.

Iman. Belief in **ALLAH** (*subhanahu wa ta'ala*), His angels, His books, His messengers, the Last Day, the divine apportionment of all things, death, life and resurrection. Belief must contextually include all of these.

Injeel. The original Gospel as revealed by **ALLAH** (*subhanahu wa ta'ala*) to the Prophet Jesus (*peace be upon him*). It is explicitly distinct from the modified "gospels" historically introduced by men under the proclamation of being "the word of God".

In Sha' ALLAH. An expression meaning, "with the Will of **ALLAH** (*subhanahu wa ta'ala*)", used when refering to events contingent upon the Will of **ALLAH** (*subhanahu wa ta'ala*).

vi

Jihad. Struggle or exertion on the Path of **ALLAH** (*subhanahu wa ta'ala*) against those forces or individuals that stand against the Way and guidance of **ALLAH** (*subhanahu wa ta'ala*). One of the main pillars of Islam, which also include prayer and fasting, etc.

Ka'aba. The cube-shaped House of **ALLAH** (*subhanahu wa ta'ala*) in Mecca. Originally built by the Prophets Abraham and Isma'il (*peace be upon them*). Muslim pilgrims visit and circumambulate this House.

Kufur. An adjective, one of whose meanings is "veiled from reality", used to refer to things or people that are not authentically Muslim. The singular noun is **kafir**, sometimes translated as "infidel". The plural is **kufar**.

Minhajan. The root of this term is **N-H-J** (**nahaja**), meaning an inductive, deductive, didactic and empirical approach, method, direction, curriculum, or apparatus that defines a basic value system in terms of its epistemology, methodology, proof and conclusions. The closest term in English is "paradigm". The title of this book in Arabic is based on this word.

Salaat. The five daily prayers that are obligatory duties for every adult Muslim. This is one of the main pillars of Islam.

Shari'ah. The Divine Law of Islam, established by **ALLAH** (*subhanahu wa ta'ala*). The root of the term is **SH-R-'A** (**shara'a**), meaning to start or initiate a path. **Shari'ah** literally means a river. Thus when a person goes through the path of **Shari'ah**, the Law is cleansing him.

vii

Shahada. The witnessing or testimony that "there is no god except **ALLAH** and **Muhammad** is the Messenger of **ALLAH**". When humanity was still in the realm of spirit, each spirit individually witnessed and promised to worship **ALLAH** (*subhanahu wa ta'ala*). He asked them, "Am I not your Lord?" All of them said "Yes!" When people say this statement in the mundane life, they are affirming what they had already witnessed. The act of saying this statement makes one a Muslim, thereby fulfilling one's original testimony that **ALLAH** (*subhanahu wa ta'ala*) is his Lord. One who says, or even hears, and lives and embodies this statement with truth and sincerity, will eventually go to Paradise.

Shaytan. Satan, the devil. The root **SH-T-N (shatana)** means to become deviant, and out of the Straight Path. The Straight Path means the shortest distance between two points. The person who adopts a value system outside this Divinely-ordained Straight Path becomes *Shaytan*. *Shaytan* is a deviant system of value "imposed" upon an individual. *Shaytan* invites the individual to deviation, but has no authority over him. *Shaytan* represents a deviant code of behavior.

Sunnah. The path trodden by our **Prophet Muhammad** (*prayers and peace of ALLAH be upon him*), his practical example of the Islamic *Din* in all aspects of speech and action.

Surah. A "chapter" of the **Generous Qur'an**. There are 114 *Surahs* in all.

Taqwa. Piety, or consciousness of **ALLAH** (*subhanahu wa ta'ala*). Its prerequisites are that a person be a true Muslim and develop true belief.

Taurat. The original tablets of the Torah, given by **ALLAH** (*subhanahu wa ta'ala*) to the Prophet Moses (*peace be upon him*). It is explicitly distinct from the modified "Torah" historically introduced by men under the proclamation of being "the word of God".

Tawhid. The absolute Oneness of **ALLAH** (*subhanahu wa ta'ala*). The existence of only One God, which means that His will and value system governs the trajectory of the world. There is no power except His.

Thikr. The root of the word is **TH-K-R**, meaning remembrance. The best remembrance is the remembrance of **ALLAH** (*subhanahu wa ta'ala*), in order that no other force will govern or influence the indivdual. **Thikr** implies that the person is only remembering what he had already learned.

Ummah. The root is **UM**, meaning "mother". **Ummah** thereby means an extended family which has embedded in it different tribes and peoples, all of which adhere to one value system and have developed the ethos of being together, building a sense of the "we", analogous to that of the family around the mother. This togetherness is the source of life and power. Only the mother can put the family together.

Usul al-din. The authentic principles of the Din of Islam that encompass a variety of disciplines.

Zabur. The original, divinely-ordained Psalms of the Prophet Daud (David, the son of Solomon, peace be upon them).

Foreward

It would be next to impossible to express the efforts that have gone into this research project. Week after week, month after month and year after year, over one full decade has been spent researching the depths of the Order of Things in general, and in particular the question of how best to convey the treasures of Islam to the world. The best approach is for Muslims to become examples *par excellence* of what Islam is all about. Thus when they write, speak and relate to others, they should follow our **Prophet Muhammad** (*prayers and peace of* **ALLAH** *be upon him*), and try their best to be forbearing. Nobody knows what tomorrow will bring, so the only course of action is to do one's best, and to know that **ALLAH** (*subhanahu wa ta'ala*) knows the hidden and outward dimensions of every human being and all things. No-one can cheat or deceive Him. This is why one should depend only on **ALLAH** (*subhanahu wa ta'ala*).

We thank **ALLAH** (*subhanahu wa ta'ala*) for providing us with the ability to dedicate ourselves to Him and to Islam, and for helping us to do our best to invite people to Islam, the only accepted *Din* (way of life) in the eyes of **ALLAH** (*subhanahu wa ta'ala*). We give our acknowledgment to my father and mother, who taught me from my youth to surrender to **ALLAH** (*subhanahu wa ta'ala*), and also to my grandfather Sheikh Salime, *Mufti Jaffa*, religious governor of Jaffa, Palestine. We are only trying to continue their works and messages.

We thank **ALLAH** (*subhanahu wa ta'ala*) for providing us with people to help us in these endeavors. We thank every person we met, whether he or she did in fact help us or rejected us, because through interacting with many individuals we learned to depend only on **ALLAH** (*subhanahu wa ta'ala*). We can assure every person that if one really surrenders to **ALLAH** (*subhanahu wa*

x

ta'ala) He will mysteriously help and lead one to His Way, enabling one to accomplish any endeavor undertaken for His Sake.

We thank **ALLAH** (*subhanahu wa ta'ala*) for helping us at every stage. Without His generous help none of this work would have been possible. He helped us through individuals who assisted us with typing and editing this book, and with arranging it according to the demands and opportunities of the Macintosh computer system. We thank **ALLAH** (*subhanahu wa ta'ala*) for having mysteriously established this system and other hi-tech apparatus that has simplified the many tasks of putting a book into finished form.

It is important here to point out that the call to Islam would be helped greatly if there are Muslims who can put the entire **Generous Qur'an**, in Arabic, on a readily available storage system that is compatible with, and accessible to, word-processing programs on the Macintosh computer. This would enhance the capabilities of Muslim writers to present in their work quotations from the **Generous Qur'an** itself, which is the fundamental basis of all Islamic scholarship.

We thank every university or school at which we either studied or taught. In addition, we are deeply indebted to *Makkah Al-Mukarramah* (Mecca) and *Madinah Al-Munawwarah* (Medina). We have learned much from being in these holy places. We learned something there that books and lectures can never convey. We learned that humanity *is* and *can be* healthy, and that it *can* unite, only under the umbrella of **ALLAH** (*subhanahu wa ta'ala*). We thank the teachers and professors that we met, in all the Muslim countries and in the United States. We have learned that every person, regardless of where he or she was born, was created by **ALLAH** (*subhanahu wa ta'ala*), and has the potential to become *'abd* **ALLAH**, the slave of **ALLAH** (*subhanahu wa ta'ala*).

xi

The Arabic, Qur'anic and Islamic Paradigm:
Light, Jewels and Pearls

Our words are too feeble to explain what has gone into this research project, whether in terms of conception, empirical reality or technical know-how. What we are dealing with is a diversity of cognitions. One of these cognitions is on the Straight Path of **ALLAH** (*subhanahu wa ta'ala*), and the others are searching, but have lost, in the course of the search, the sharp edge of discrepancy. In no way could we put those who know and those who do not know on the same footing. Calling to Islam requires that a person understand the fiber and fabric of the non-Islamic cognition, and deal with that cognition according to the practice of our beloved **Prophet Muhammad** (*prayers and peace of* **ALLAH** *be upon him*).

We feel that when scholars do research, they are doing only one of two things. Either they are simply lining up letters and words without a real or transcendent conception, thereby declaring their pluralistic ignorance, or they are asserting certain reality, reality that constitutes the abiding force of history. The latter can be no other than the authentic Word of **ALLAH** (*subhanahu wa ta'ala*). When a person wants to study the Word of **ALLAH** (*subhanahu wa ta'ala*), a journey is required. It is not a journey of a day, a week or a decade; it is an eternal journey. It is the most beautiful journey that can ever be taken. ·

We dedicate our lives to **ALLAH** (*subhanahu wa ta'ala*), and therefore all of our work is for **ALLAH** (*subhanahu wa ta'ala*). We ask **ALLAH** (*subhanahu wa ta'ala*) to make this work only for Him, and to make us committed to understanding the mystery of His Word. Only by total surrender can this be achieved. We are seeking neither fame nor wealth. We are simply the slaves of **ALLAH** (*subhanahu wa ta'ala*).

If some people think, for one reason or another, that we have not been correct in our endeavor, we ask them to ask **ALLAH** (*subhanahu wa ta'ala*) to guide us to the Straight Path. We have done our best, and we are continuing to do our best. **ALLAH** (*subhanahu wa ta'ala*) will do the rest. This manuscript has been written several times. Each time it was ready to be printed, we reviewed and corrected it again, because we found that learning is a constant journey of change. We acknowledge that there are still mistakes in this book, because no-one is perfect except **ALLAH** (*subhanahu wa ta'ala*). We have tried to keep our wordings simple, but in trying to be objective, one has to use certain concepts and terms which fit a multiplicity of understandings, yet do not violate the contextual manifestation of reality.

We have tried to be conscious of our use of language in many ways. For example, we would always prefer, when referring to humanity in general, and to individuals in a broad sense, not to use language that could be construed as sexist. We have done our best on this count, but the reader should understand that if on certain occasions we say "he" rather than "he or she", or "mankind" rather than "humankind", we are meaning to indicate people of both genders. Finally, we discovered that the term "word" can have different and subtle implications depending on capitalization and other variables. It should be understood that we tried to capitalize "Word" when we were referring to the Divine Word in a general sense, and used the uncapitalized form when referring to specific words of any kind.

In conclusion, we ask **ALLAH** (*subhanahu wa ta'ala*) to guide us and to guide all the Muslims, and all humanity, to His Straight Path. We ask Him to let us see righteousness as righteousness, and become the embodiment of righteousness, and to let us see falsehood as falsehood, and to protect us from it. We can summarize all this in one phrase. "Please, Lord, help us to be Your slaves." This is because whatever your Lord *is*, you are *his*.

و مآ ارسلناک الا رحمة للعالمين

CHAPTER I

The Generous Qur'an:
Light, Jewels and Pearls

The human word in any language is too feeble to explain the infinite reality of the **Generous Qur'an.** An exception to this is the word of our beloved **Prophet Muhammad** (*prayers and peace of* **ALLAH** *be upon him*). This is because he was not speaking on his own. He was totally under the guidance of **ALLAH's** (*subhanahu wa ta'ala*) revelation, and only **ALLAH** (*subhanahu wa ta'ala*) knows the full conception of the **Generous Qur'an.** Scholars can only offer their interpretation and perspective, after which they should say, "only **ALLAH** (*subhanahu wa ta'ala*) knows best". This is what objectivity is all about, because as a norm human understanding can only be subjective.

The **Generous Qur'an** is the only authentic, divinely-ordained book that has survived through the melodrama of the creation. **ALLAH** (*subhanahu wa ta'ala*) made a commitment to Himself to preserve it. There is no other book in history that kept its total autonomy, its conception and its meaning through time. In regard to the **Generous Qur'an**, one must understand that we are not referring to human words or human deliberation. We are referring to the Words of **ALLAH** (*subhanahu wa ta'ala*), Who created this world out of

1

Chapter I. The Generous Qur'an: Light, Jewels and Pearls

nothingness. Through His Word, creation came. Created things are thus no more than Words of **ALLAH** (*subhanahu wa ta'ala*). The **Generous Qur'an** is therefore a medium of creation, and it is indeed generous.

ALLAH (*subhanahu wa ta'ala*) is the Light of the Heavens and the Earth. Thereby, His Word is the Light of the Heavens and the Earth. His Light is infinite, and therefore His Word is infinite. Though the **Generous Qur'an** is allegorically contained in a book, this Book is infinite. Allegorically, the Book becomes a linkage between the finite and the infinite. In actuality, it is infinite. The **Generous Qur'an** is simple, yet very abstract. It is empirical in its diametrics, yet it is very conceptual in its context. It is precise in its specific indications, yet it is infinite in its meanings. It is simple and straight without any crookedness. It has told us the realities of the past, the present and the future. The trajectory of reality in itself comes to confirm the Word. This is because reality in itself came through the word. Therefore, the **Generous Qur'an** is not speculative but is reality in itself. Simply put, it is a *praxis*.

The **Generous Qur'an** is infinite Light. This Light is constituted by words in Arabic. The meaning starts with the word, and the word becomes a linkage between negation and existence. These words are inimitable and have been preserved from before the beginning until after the end; that is, before the alpha and after the omega. These words of light have imbedded within them infinite realities and secrets. **ALLAH** (*subhanahu wa ta'ala*) refers to the **Qur'an** as being generous. This generosity is in a hidden book, meaning that it contains in the words themselves infinite secrets and mysteries of life, and it guides us in deciphering and decoding reality. This is contingent upon that the reader makes a total surrender to **ALLAH** (*subhanahu wa ta'ala*)

2

Chapter I. The Generous Qur'an: Light, Jewels and Pearls

and thereby becomes a true believer. At that point, the Light of **ALLAH** (*subhanahu wa ta'ala*) will be given to that person so that he or she can understand some of the secrets of these words. These secrets are jewels and pearls. No human intellect's words could ever substitute the **Generous Qur'an's** words. This is because these words are Light within words. These Words will shed Light on the reciter of the **Generous Qur'an**. Thereby, they will become secrets inside the jewels and pearls. In reality, nothing is hidden about them, because these jewels and pearls shine so brightly and clearly. This is why they crystallize what they are, stunning their audience. Everything declares itself by itself.

There is no doubt that jewelers understand jewelry. If a person puts jewels, pearls and glass marbles together, many people cannot distinguish the jewels and pearls from the marbles. Thus an individual who surrenders his life to the Lord, and has actually learned and became the embodiment of the *Shari'atu* **ALLAH** (*subhanahu wa ta'ala*) (the Law of God) and the true *Sunnah* (the *praxis* of the **Prophet Muhammad**--*prayers and peace of* **ALLAH** *be upon him*), might be able to understand the value of the treasures in the **Generous Qur'an**. Its words cannot be duplicated by any human being. Thereby, when a person wants to convey this treasure to people that do not understand, and have no tradition of appreciating its lights, jewels and pearls, he has to consider the cognition, the station and the level of his audience. Sometimes, he has to learn the lexicon and the terms that his audience uses, and learn how to speak on their level. This does not mean that he should try to reduce the light, jewels and pearls of the **Generous Qur'an** to that level, but only that he should educate and therapeutically prepare the audience, with congeniality, so they may start to appreciate the treasures and the Light that are embedded in the

Chapter I. The Generous Qur'an: Light, Jewels and Pearls

Generous Qur'an, contingent upon **ALLAH's** (*subhanahu wa ta'ala*) permission.

Today, we are witnessing in the whole spaceship earth a veiled and enveloped "civilization" that is governed by a value system other than authentic Islam. This "civilization" takes pride in proclaiming to have developed its analytical mind, and glorifies the "goddess of reason". Paradoxically, it ends up worshipping itself, because it was lured by *Shaytan* (Satan). Thereby, it becomes encapsulated within the illusionary interplay between space and time. It becomes anesthetized by its own might.

The authors are trying, with all good intentions, to follow the method of our **Prophet Muhammad** (*prayers and peace of* **ALLAH** *be upon him*) in inviting the non-Muslims to Islam. **ALLAH** (*subhanahu wa ta'ala*) sent our **Prophet Muhammad** (*prayers and peace of* **ALLAH** *be upon him*) to the heart of *Makkah Al-Mukarramah* (Mecca). While he spoke the language of the Arabs, a language which they could relate to and cognitively understand, he did not conform to their value system. Also, the Prophet Jesus (*peace be upon him*), son of the virgin Mary, who was endorsed with the Holy Spirit, tried to invite people with congeniality by teaching them the highest form of forgiveness. For example, when the crowd was ready to stone Mary Magdalene in Jerusalem, the Holy City of peace, he said that the person who was without mistakes should throw the first stone. In addition, the Prophet Moses (*peace be upon him*) was ordered to go to Pharaoh and speak gently and congenially with him, using lenient language, in the anticipation that Pharaoh might remember his Lord and be guided. The point is that, if you want to invite a person to your house, you must offer your best to him in a very congenial manner. This is the prophetic approach of calling to Islam.

The Arabic, Qur'anic and Islamic Paradigm:
Light, Jewels and Pearls

Chapter I. The Generous Qur'an: Light, Jewels and Pearls

This exposé, under the title of *The Arabic, Qur'anic and Islamic Paradigm : Light, Jewels and Pearls*, is no more than an indigenous call to Islam. The **Generous Qur'an** is indeed Light, jewels, pearls and other treasures. In no way could one say that these treasures could have synonyms in any other language. This is simply because **ALLAH** (*subhanahu wa ta'ala*), Who created us out of nothingness, revealed the **Generous Qur'an**, His authentic Word, in the Arabic language. There is no more valuable activity in the world than to believe in, learn, study and practice the Word of the Lord, **ALLAH** (*subhanahu wa ta'ala*).

Historically, scholars came from all corners of the world, to centers of erudition and light in Basrah, Kufah, Baghdad, Makkah Al-Mukarramah, Medina Al-Munawwarah, Jerusalem, Damascus, Cairo (Al-Azhar), Tunis (Jame'a Zaytounah), Fes (Al-Qarawiyin) and other places, in the anticipation of learning the Arabic language and understanding the **Generous Qur'an** in Arabic. Many Islamic scholars were originally not Arabs, but they learned Arabic in order to read the **Generous Qur'an**. They wrote books about Islam in Arabic. One of the leading scholars was Abu Hamid Al-Ghazali (who was born in the year 450 A.H./1058 A.D. and died in the year 505 A.H./1111 A.D.). He wrote many erudite volumes, including *The Jewels of the Qur'an*. He was a Persian from Khorasan, but he wrote in Arabic.

All Muslims are considered to be brothers and sisters who are united in surrender to the Lord. Arabism is not a fanatic nationalistic movement, because in authentic Islam there is no nationalism. The **Prophet Muhammad** (*prayers and peace of* **ALLAH** *be upon him*) said in an authentic *hadith* (narrated saying) what could be conceptually articulated to mean that "Any person who speaks Arabic is an Arab". The authentic Islamic community is not based on any type of racial or ethnic biases or differentiation. **ALLAH** (*subhanahu wa ta'ala*) told us in

5

the **Generous Qur'an** that He has created humanity from one essence, that He made us to be of different genders, peoples and tribes so that we could be oriented to each other, and that the best of us in the view of **ALLAH** (*subhanahu wa ta'ala*) are those that have piety. No person could develop piety without believing in **ALLAH** (*subhanahu wa ta'ala*) and following the Light brought through His **Prophet Muhammad** (*prayers and peace of* **ALLAH** *be upon him*), loving and recognizing the latter's status as the highest of God's messengers and prophets. Piety requires, among other variables, being a Muslim, praying in Arabic and reading the **Generous Qur'an** in Arabic as a guiding force.

This is why the authors have tried their best to look for the original **Qur'anic** verses, introduce and deliberate about them within a contextual Arabic, Qur'anic and Islamic methodology. In addition, our frame of reference in its fibre and fabric, with the will of **ALLAH** (*subhanahu wa ta'ala*), is epistemologically based on the Islamic cognition. Only **ALLAH** (*subhanahu wa ta'ala*) knows the years of effort that have gone into this work. What we are trying to do is to stand for **ALLAH** (*subhanahu wa ta'ala*), and only **ALLAH** (*subhanahu wa ta'ala*) can reward us.

It is important that we recognize our limitations. We cannot come close to saying that we have made a "rigorous" exposé, because only **ALLAH** (*subhanahu wa ta'ala*), and not we, can judge. We deliberately do not use the term "conceptual framework", because only **ALLAH** (*subhanahu wa ta'ala*) knows best the infinite meaning of His Word. What He says is perfect, and we willingly accept His Judgement. We know for sure that He is better to us than we can be to ourselves. We are vehement and enthusiastically His slaves (*"abd* **ALLAH"**). Whatever your Lord *is*, you are *his*.

6

The Arabic, Qur'anic and Islamic Paradigm:
Light, Jewels and Pearls

Chapter I. The Generous Qur'an: Light, Jewels and Pearls

Human deliberation and consciousness cannot encompass God's consciousness. The opposite is in fact true, because **ALLAH** (*subhanahu wa ta'ala*) invades and navigates through the hearts of His true believers. This is no more than an attempt, in a simple style, to invite those whom **ALLAH** (*subhanahu wa ta'ala*) gives permission to follow His Way. They must be reminded in a delicate and profound manner that their ways are not the example *par excellence* of straightness, healthiness and openness. Simultaneously, they must be introduced to Islam as a *modus operandi* and *modus vivendi* to strip them of deviation and rectify them to their original essence.

Islam has the light and the treasure in the form of the **Generous Qur'an**. The latter is the way, the light and the truth. It contains jewels and pearls that can never be duplicated by any human. This is why people should learn the Arabic language in the anticipation of reading the **Generous Qur'an** in Arabic. They should try to believe in and to live by the teaching of the **Generous Qur'an** and the authentic *Sunnah* of our beloved **Prophet Muhammad** (*prayers and peace of* **ALLAH** *be upon him*) in all realms, including their *modus operandi* and *modus vivendi*. They should glorify **ALLAH** (*subhanahu wa ta'ala*) and venerate His beloved Arabian **Prophet Muhammad** (*prayers and peace of* **ALLAH** *be upon him*), the World-Light-Splendor.

In and between the following lines, the Light, the jewels and the pearls of the **Generous Qur'an** will be demonstrated in the authentic Islamic methodology of negation followed by affirmation. As a result, the exposé is articulated in such a delicate and profound manner that it will take a dedicated, conscious individual to understand it, after which **ALLAH** (*subhanahu wa ta'ala*) might give him the permission to surrender to Him in Islam and receive guidance. What your Lord *is*, you are *his*. This book has to be read from the heart and with care.

7

Chapter I. The Generous Qur'an: Light, Jewels and Pearls

Empirical Abstracted Reality

In the proliferation of literature in the fields of all realms of reality, such as linguistics, religion, culture, history, politics, physics, chemistry and others, there have been few attempts at an analytical synthesis to explain reality based upon Islamic methodology. Islamic methodology has already been established by **ALLAH** (*subhanahu wa ta'ala*) and His beloved **Prophet Muhammad** (*prayers and peace of* **ALLAH** *be upon him*). Therefore, the Islamic *Din, pari passu*, methodology, a *modus operandi* for *modus vivendi*, is divinely-ordained, and has been guaranteed protection and preservation by **ALLAH** (*subhanahu wa ta'ala*). The Islamic methodology is not a theoretical abstraction resulting from speculative notions of reality, but it is a *de facto* reality that governs the hidden and the apparent dimensions of the order of things. The notions of reality of the *kufur*, (veiled) West and East, and others (i.e. non-Muslims) is based on so-called scientific, speculative assumptions.   These can change over time, because man is encapsulated within the illusionary interplay of space and time. The "science" of today can become the "ignoble lie" of tomorrow. As well, the lies of today can become the science of tomorrow. The different scientific theories are not an example par excellence for understanding reality. Nevertheless they may play only an auxiliary, transient and short-lived role. Thereby, they constitute no more than the changing variables of history. Islam gave us holistic and holy realities. It is divinely-ordained, and thereby it is compatible with and accountable to, yet transcendent of, every epoch of history. Therefore, it constitutes the abiding forces of history. This is why it is auto-legitimating.

Scientific speculation, on the other hand, lacks the semi-balance of legitimacy. Within this context, the servant researchers and writers of

8

The Arabic, Qur'anic and Islamic Paradigm:
Light, Jewels and Pearls

Chapter I. The Generous Qur'an: Light, Jewels and Pearls

this exposé are doing no more than explaining reality based on Islamic methodology. In circles that are not authentically Islamic, methodologies for approaching Islam are victims of and enveloped within the phenomenon of compartmentalization, and have usually ignored the importance of a broadened view establishing a trans- and intra-disciplinary vision of reality. That cannot be done without going back to the **Generous Qur'an**, the divinely-ordained book, as well as the *praxis* of the **Prophet Muhammad** (*prayers and peace of* **ALLAH** *be upon him*).

Regardless of how vehemently a non-Muslim theorist believes in his epistemological absolute value system, it has to be understood that whatever he has constructed is no more than a speculative notion of reality, because humankind can only know a part of the apparent reality. Whatever his experimentation, observation and conceptualization lead him to, they do not lead him to a total, absolute reality. This is applicable whether the method is inductive or deductive, and/or paradigmatic. The issue here is that the theorist who is not an authentic Muslim has a frame of reference that is not **ALLAH** (*subhanahu wa ta'ala*). Thereby, in his intellectual deliberation, he is not guided by **ALLAH's** (*subhanahu wa ta'ala*) vision. He is not remembering **ALLAH** (*subhanahu wa ta'ala*). As a result, for a person who is not remembering **ALLAH** (*subhanahu wa ta'ala*), and whose frame of reference is not **ALLAH** (*subhanahu wa ta'ala*), his or her epistemological absolute value is something other than **ALLAH** (*subhanahu wa ta'ala*). When a person's intellectual apparatus and vision are not based on **ALLAH's** (*subhanahu wa ta'ala*) value system, such as the *Shari'ah* and the *Sunnah*, the bases of creation, the *modus operandi* and *modus vivendi* of Islam, etc., that person becomes vulnerable to *Shaytan's* (Satan's) luring technique. *Shaytan* starts to

9

Chapter I. The Generous Qur'an: Light, Jewels and Pearls

let the person see things with an apparent conceptual clarity to the point that he or she becomes veiled from reality. Paradoxically, such a person feels guided. People of this quasi-intellectual prototype are worshipping their theories, and thereby are totally kidnapped from their true, indigenous essence, as well as from the holistic and holy reality. The Lord will provide for them whatever they want from this mundane life, including silver roofs and ornaments of gold. This would represent only a provision of this life, but the provision of the Hereafter is much better, and will be for those who keep away from evil. If they follow truncated vision, which is a type of "light" other than that given by **ALLAH** (*subhanahu wa ta'ala*), people are asserting that they are blind. Those who are blind to truth in this life, regardless of how much they glorify their theories, will also be blind in the next life, and even worse. Thereby, **ALLAH** (*subhanahu wa ta'ala*) will creep up on them from corners that they never anticipated, and destroy their theories from the bases of their legitimacy. Every theory has been destroyed, whether it was a Marxist-Leninist, Durkheimian, Parsonian, structural-functionalist, social-linguistic, anthropological, Freudian, existentialist, Leo Straussian, free-market-capitalist, welfare-state or corporatist theory, etc. All of these and other theories constitute no more than a particularistic perspective of reality articulated in universalistic terms. The inversion of the particular to the universal and the universal to the particular has been manifested in the attempt to establish the rule and sovereignty of man over the earth, rather than the rule and sovereignty of God. Thereby, **ALLAH** (*subhanahu wa ta'ala*) declares war upon the adherents of these particularistic, deviant, crooked ways, because they are challenging the Straight Way of **ALLAH** (*subhanahu wa ta'ala*) in His domain. **ALLAH** (*subhanahu wa ta'ala*) has made a commitment upon Himself to establish His Way, *pari*

10

Chapter I. The Generous Qur'an: Light, Jewels and Pearls

passu, the Islamic *Din* on the whole earth, even though the infidels may hate, reject and fight it. There is no victory except **ALLAH's** (*subhanahu wa ta'ala*) victory.

This is because these non-authentic-Muslim theorists and their followers and prototypes did not vehemently start their epistemology with true belief in **ALLAH** (*subhanahu wa ta'ala*), and they did not remember Him in their method. At that point, (as indicated in the following excerpt from the **Generous Qur'an**, *Surah Al-Zukhruf*, XLIII, verses 36 and 37) **ALLAH** (*subhanahu wa ta'ala*) appoints for each of them a *Shaytan* who dwells in their truncated analytical vision, causing them to try to hypothesize "rigorous" modeling systems. Their vision becomes saturated with a secondary and imposed, not indigenous, nature. Their indigenous nature is to search for the truth, and to search for their Lord in every aspect of every discipline, including chemistry and physics, etc. Paradoxically, when their epistemological frame of reference is not **ALLAH** (*subhanahu wa ta'ala*), then they have been willingly kidnapped by a *Shaytanic* comrade, though he has no authority over them. As a result, they become *Shaytanic* prototypes.

Thuluth

"Nun, by the pen and that which they write"

11

****

SURAH XLIII (43) *Ornaments
of Gold*

33. And were it not that mankind would have become one community, We might well have appointed, for those who disbelieve in the Beneficent, roofs of silver for their houses and stairs (of silver) whereby to mount,

وَلَوْلَا أَن يَكُونَ النَّاسُ أُمَّةً وَاحِدَةً لَجَعَلْنَا لِمَن يَكْفُرُ بِالرَّحْمَٰنِ لِبُيُوتِهِمْ سُقُفًا مِّن فِضَّةٍ وَمَعَارِجَ عَلَيْهَا يَظْهَرُونَ ۝

34. And for their houses doors (of silver) and couches of silver whereon to recline,

وَلِبُيُوتِهِمْ أَبْوَابًا وَسُرُرًا عَلَيْهَا يَتَّكِئُونَ ۝

35. And ornaments of gold. Yet all that would have been but a provision of the life of the world. And the Hereafter with your Lord would have been for those who keep from evil.

وَزُخْرُفًا وَإِن كُلُّ ذَٰلِكَ لَمَّا مَتَاعُ الْحَيَاةِ الدُّنْيَا وَالْآخِرَةُ عِندَ رَبِّكَ لِلْمُتَّقِينَ ۝

36. And he whose sight is dim to the remembrance of the Beneficent, We assign unto him a devil who becometh his comrade;

وَمَن يَعْشُ عَن ذِكْرِ الرَّحْمَٰنِ نُقَيِّضْ لَهُ شَيْطَانًا فَهُوَ لَهُ قَرِينٌ ۝

37. And Lo! they surely turn them from the way of Allah, and yet they deem that they are rightly guided.

وَإِنَّهُمْ لَيَصُدُّونَهُمْ عَنِ السَّبِيلِ وَيَحْسَبُونَ أَنَّهُم مُّهْتَدُونَ ۝

XLIII *Surah Al-Zukhruf*, **The Generous Qur'an** 43:33-37

****

12

The Arabic, Qur'anic and Islamic Paradigm:
Light, Jewels and Pearls

Chapter I. The Generous Qur'an: Light, Jewels and Pearls

The authors feel vehemently that the non-authentic-Islamic intellectual apparatus that exists today in various circles in the East and West, and all over the world, is enveloped within the illusionary interplay between space and time. Thereby, its adherents cannot see reality *in toto* as an independent variable, in its holistic and holy dimensions. What they are seeing are analytical, speculative notions of reality that are a result of human-concocted assumptions and "laws". Paradoxically, they start to see things with clarity and with a certain limited analytical "light", to the point that this "light" blinds them. They ended up glorifying their theories, and started to worship them. What they were actually involved in was self-glorification, and thereby they tried to elevate themselves to the level of sovereignty through worship of the "goddess of reason". The result was an attempt to establish the rule and the sovereignty of man over man. **ALLAH** (*subhanahu wa ta'ala*) never tolerates that anything be worshipped and glorified except Him. Thus, He creeps up on them from corners they never anticipated. Every theory has crumbled, been destroyed and vanished. Only the **Generous Qur'an** and the true *Sunnah* have been preserved.

We feel that some of these quasi-intellectuals are searching, but we believe that they are extremely primitive and are lost in the darkness. This might be for several reasons, some of which include the following. Perhaps they simply refused to believe in the divinely-ordained Word of **ALLAH** (*subhanahu wa ta'ala*), the **Generous Qur'an** and the true *Sunnah*. Perhaps their scholarship was not educatively transformed by it, making them the embodiment of the Law of **ALLAH** (*subhanahu wa ta'ala*). Perhaps they were misguided about it by others. There might be other reasons. This research is just for these people in particular, and for all people in general, in the anticipation that the

13

The Arabic, Qur'anic and Islamic Paradigm:
Light, Jewels and Pearls

Chapter I. The Generous Qur'an: Light, Jewels and Pearls

readers who need it might strip themselves of truncated vision which has been socially inculcated in them, and has caused them to be anesthetized and in a state of heedlessness.

It is imperative to understand that Islam is not a theory. We are not trying to construct something new in this research. The emphasis lies on asserting something that is already there. This is why we dedicated ourselves for many years to including the **Generous Qur'anic** verses in Arabic. Those verses in Arabic are the authentic Word of **ALLAH** (*subhanahu wa ta'ala*), while the English translations/interpretations of them are not, though they might play an auxiliary role. The reader who is not privileged to understand Arabic might still read the English and be guided by **ALLAH** (*subhanahu wa ta'ala*) to reality, with the Will of **ALLAH** (*subhanahu wa ta'ala*). We are using English terms only to convey to the unprivileged individuals, who do not understand Arabic, certain **Qur'anic** perceptions.

We never intended to build a paradigm, because the Islamic way and methodology has already been established. We use the term in the anticipation that the readers might really be enlightened. The first step in enlightenment is to strip the self of theories and self-glorification. We are using standard terms in the anticipation that readers might see reality based on a divinely-ordained conception of **Qur'anic** verses. If at one place or another, we use a term that explicitly indicates the concepts of building, modeling, or constructing a paradigm, etc., we only mean that we are pointing to what already exists in the divinely-ordained **Generous Qur'an** in Arabic and in the authentic *hadith*. We are using these terms just to convey, with the help of **ALLAH** (*subhanahu wa ta'ala*), the profound eloquence of His Straight Way, the Islamic *Din*. The word in English becomes too feeble for totally

14

The Arabic, Qur'anic and Islamic Paradigm: Light, Jewels and Pearls

Chapter I. The Generous Qur'an: Light, Jewels and Pearls

conveying **ALLAH's** (*subhanahu wa ta'ala*) Word in Arabic, either in its conception or in its inimitable, majesty beauty.

There is a great need for articulating the authentically Islamic paradigm in English and/or other non-Arabic languages, using the **Generous Qur'an** and the Arabic language for an understanding of Islamic belief and *praxis*. In particular, there needs to be a paradigmatic framework through which the unique perspective of Islam can be introduced and heard across cultural, linguistic, scientific and other contexts. This does not mean that a person must be a Muslim in order to read this book. From the Islamic perspective, every person is a Muslim at birth, and it is social inculcation that deviates him from his original essence. A non-Muslim might search for reality in any dimension of science, himself or the universe. Through his observations, **ALLAH** (*subhanahu wa ta'ala*) might lead him. The universe in itself, as well as the individual himself, constitutes signs of the majestic existence of God. When a person reads this book, it might clarify certain things in the anticipation that God will rectify him to his true essence, which is Islam. Every person, regardless of who he or she is is a result of **ALLAH's** (*subhanahu wa ta'ala*) creation.

The heart of Islam is science, and the first verse of the **Generous Qur'an** that was revealed concerned knowledge. To understand Islam, one cannot only use human-concocted laws as analytical devices. To understand any reality, one should start with Islamic belief and the **Qur'anic** methodology as a tool of analysis. That implies an objectivity in the method. Simply put, the Word of **ALLAH** (*subhanahu wa ta'ala*), as it was divinely-ordained in the **Generous Qur'an** in Arabic, is the first place to start. In the **Qur'anic** word, phrase and sentence is the simple method, because it is easily understood by the average individual. In the course of the individual's metamorphosis, complexities start to reveal themselves through these simple words.

15

The Arabic, Qur'anic and Islamic Paradigm:
Light, Jewels and Pearls

Chapter I. The Generous Qur'an: Light, Jewels and Pearls

The authors have been engaged in a continuous research project directed at the relationship of Islam and life in contemporary society, a society that is increasingly taking on global dimensions partly as a result of the spread of scientific and technological perspectives and apparatus. This research has had its starting point and perpetual center in the **Generous Qur'an** itself. The urgent issue that has arisen has been an incommensurability between the Islamic foundations of the **Generous Qur'an** and the *Sunnah* of our beloved Arabian **Prophet Muhammad** (*prayers and peace of* **ALLAH** *be upon him*), and the various theoretical constructs usually used in analysis and discourse in the *kufur* (non-authentic-Islamic) academic institutions of the East and the West. The authors have found it necessary to articulate and point out a framework or paradigm through which to communicate across this line of incommensurability. This is based on the **Generous Qur'an**, and the authors are not adding or bringing anything new. The result is an attempt to introduce readers of many perspectives to a paradigmatic background from which to begin looking at the topic of Islam and its relation to life, science and language in contemporary society. An essential preliminary stage in this discussion is to delimit precisely what is meant by the term "paradigm".

بسم الله **The Holistic and Holy Concept of "Paradigm" in Islam**

In reading the **Generous Qur'an**, one finds that **ALLAH** (*subhanahu wa ta'ala*) has delineated and conjugated an answer to every aspect of life. Islam, therefore, is not a theory, because theories speculate about certain segments of life and forget others. **ALLAH** (*subhanahu wa ta'ala*), as the Creator, is in a better position to tell us what should be done. Simply put, Islam is a way of life, a *modus*

Chapter I. The Generous Qur'an: Light, Jewels and Pearls

operandi for *modus vivendi*. This way constitutes a simple, empirical, yet abstract approach to life. The **Qur'anic** verse in itself becomes a polymetric linkage between the abstract and the empirical. Each verse is very simple, and could be understood by any sane person who has a basic knowledge of the Arabic language. That individual's understanding is related to his cognition as well as his dedicated *praxis* of Islam. Therefore, the individual becomes the medium between the infinite, abstract meaning and the simple, verbatim verse.

The individual will understand according to what light **ALLAH** (*subhanahu wa ta'ala*) gives him. Nevertheless the conceptual meaning understood by each person is contingent upon the work of the dedicated scholars who are deeply and well trained in the basics of the Islamic *Din*, who can suggest a perspective of the demarcation line in each contextual, non-disputed issue. In Islam, the scholarly individual gives an opinion and in the final analysis he or she says "God knows best". In Islam, true scholars do not theorize, meaning that they do not construct something new to add to Islam. Nevertheless, they deliberate according to the Islamic approach and didactics. In the *kufur* West and East, there are many theories. Through time, scholars know that these theories are bankrupt. As a result, they either reject or modify them. Thereby they become modificationists, because their theories did not encompass reality, whereas Islam is a divinely-ordained reality, *fait accompli*. Authentic Muslim scholars are involved, not in theorizing about Islam, but in *praxis* of Islam, in the anticipation of acquiring *taqwa* (piety). When a person has piety, he can read the **Generous Qur'an** as a guiding force. At that point he sees the same verse in a different, "infinite" light, to the point that he really surrenders. He transfers from the realm of understanding the verse (and no person can really understand its conception *in toto*), to the realm of admiration and surrender, with a strong belief, to His Majesty,

17

Chapter I. The Generous Qur'an: Light, Jewels and Pearls

ALLAH (*subhanahu wa ta'ala*). The method of understanding and deliberating in Islam constitutes a divinely-ordained method. Thereby it is the abiding force of history. **ALLAH** (*subhanahu wa ta'ala*), (in the **Generous Qur'an**, *Surah Al-Ma'ida*, V, The Table Spread, verse 48) calls that method *minhaja*. The closest concept in English to this word is "paradigm". However, the meaning of *minhaja* in Islam is different from the customary analytical meaning of "paradigm" in the non-Muslim Western and Eastern professional circles and tradition. مِنْهَاجًا

The Non-Muslim Concept of Paradigm

It is imperative to understand that from the Islamic perspective of reality, a non-guided person, pari passu, a non-Muslim, is a person who does not have the real Light of **ALLAH** (*subhanahu wa ta'ala*). Therefore, that person is enveloped and veiled within the illusionary interplay between space and time. This is why a notion that is non-Islamic is called *kufur*, meaning veiled. The term "paradigm" from the *kufur* Western and Eastern perspective represents a changing conception. This is because the adherents of this perspective are extremely primitive, as they had not been selected by the Lord to be carriers of a divinely-ordained, messianic message. Thereby, they become carriers of a lower, mundane message that is a product of their notions of reality which are not divinely-ordained. Therefore, their laws become transitional and contemporaneous. Their paradigms become the changing variables of history. In the process, they have lost the demarcation line between what is good and what is bad, and their concepts of morality and immorality become intermingled. This happens to the point that, through the proclamation of "majority rule", where the majority never actually rules, cats become dogs and dogs

18

The Arabic, Qur'anic and Islamic Paradigm: Light, Jewels and Pearls

Chapter I. The Generous Qur'an: Light, Jewels and Pearls

become cats. By the same token, what constitutes man becomes what constitutes woman, and vice versa, through the pretense of "human rights" and the concepts of the nuclear family and "unisex". Thereby, these people forget that the Lord created Adam and Eve, not Adam and Steve. The point is that they are worshipping different idols at every epoch of history. Each theorist carries his own idol. Marxists, for example carry the idol of Marx, while the Durkheimians carry the idol of Durkheim, and the Parsonians carry the idol of Talcott Parsons. This is similar to the situation in Mecca prior to the appearance of our beloved Arabian **Prophet Muhammad** (*prayers and peace of* **ALLAH** *be upon him*), the World-Light-Splendor, when each tribe built and worshipped its own idols. The tribes constructed their idols out of different materials. One tribe made an idol out of dates, and in a time of hunger they ate their "god". This era was called the Epoch of Ignorance. Our beloved Arabian **Prophet Muhammad** (*prayers and peace of* **ALLAH** *be upon him*) came and took the Arabs who became Muslims from darkness to light.

The non-Muslim theorists who construct paradigms are continuously suffering from cognitive dissonance, because their conceptualizations, assumptions and theories are incongruent with the empirical reality. This is why they are declaring their pluralistic ignorance, and they dwell in darkness, because whatever your Lord *is*, you are *his*. None of them has real knowledge. Thereby they are not really praying in their endeavors; they are spraying, in order to appear to be something that they are not, because their god is something that it is not.

The term "paradigm" has been used in a variety of ways in the non-Muslim West and East by many writers, especially in the social sciences. In defining the precise sense in which the term is to be used in this book, it is necessary first to distinguish it from other usages.

19

Copyright © 1991 by Drs. H. & J. El-Yacoubi. ALL RIGHTS RESERVED.
P.O. Box 4094 Boulder, Colorado 80306 U.S.A.

The Arabic, Qur'anic and Islamic Paradigm:
Light, Jewels and Pearls

Chapter I. The Generous Qur'an: Light, Jewels and Pearls

In some cases in the Western context, a paradigm is considered to be a conceptual model that is understood to represent a segment or aspect of "reality". That is to say, since reality cannot be approached or understood directly and as a whole system, it can be "modelled" on the basis of a limited human understanding. Through use of "paradigms" in this sense, scientists have proclaimed an understanding of how systems work in the real world, while what is really operative in the paradigm is a set of dislocated human conceptions standing in the place of reality. The result is a body of hypothesized relationships among certain variables. This body is taken as a representation of the dynamics of how the world actually works. Examples of paradigms that functioned in this way are the "structural-functional" paradigm and the "system analysis" paradigm.[1]

When a paradigm takes on a set of more directly stated propositions, it becomes known as a "theory". Thomas Kuhn, in his book, *The Structure of Scientific Revolutions*, stated that mundane constructions such as paradigms and theories tend to follow a life cycle in which their credibility is undermined from their very inception by extra-systematic events. Ultimately, as the world proves more subtle and mysterious than can be explained within a given paradigm, the paradigm itself crumbles like an idol. At this point, it is usually replaced by another paradigm in which other variables and hypothetical relationships are described. The result is an on-going cycle of paradigmatic construction and destruction, which is not bringing people any closer to an accurate and truly useful understanding of things.[2] The collapsing paradigm is no more than vain hypothesizing about illusion, and the transitional and coming paradigms are the same, because they are not epistemologically based

20

Chapter I. The Generous Qur'an: Light, Jewels and Pearls

on the value system of true belief in **ALLAH** (*subhanahu wa ta'ala*). Therefore, they lack the Light of **ALLAH** (*subhanahu wa ta'ala*). When **ALLAH** (*subhanahu wa ta'ala*) does not give someone light, that person has no light. That is to say, he is drowning in vanity, making theories and paradigms about himself, to glorify himself, rather than the Lord. This is why every such paradigm eventually decays and withers away because the Lord creeps up on its adherents from corners they never anticipated. Its methodologies start to collapse because it cannot explain or address "the real issue".

In the sense that it has been described above, a "paradigm" can be taken to refer to a very limited, contemporaneous and ultimately futile approach to reality. It is important to understand that this is not the sense in which the authors of this book are using the term. The authentic Islamic paradigm (*minhaja*) discussed here is to be understood as incommensurable with any other type of paradigm. This is what is called *tawhid* (Oneness). What the approach involves is not a tentative set of hypotheses and research questions. Rather, it is an attempt, through a discussion of some crucial empirical variables, to portray with a degree of fullness and depth some of the infinite dynamism of Islamic belief and *praxis*. The latter reflects an integrated and infinitely applicable framework for human life under the guidance of **ALLAH** (*subhanahu wa ta'ala*). The crucial variables to be discussed in the book are the Arabic language, the **Generous Qur'an** itself, and their role in the Islamic way of life, as it involves a "paradigm" for belief and *praxis*.

21

Chapter I. The Generous Qur'an: Light, Jewels and Pearls

The Spectrum and Methodology of the Study

As a preliminary, since the **Generous Qur'an** descended in Arabic, it is necessary to discuss the uniqueness of the Arabic language as a prelude to an accurate discussion of the role of the **Generous Qur'an**. The **Generous Qur'an** itself is the ultimate frame of reference for Islamic belief and *praxis*. Social relations are stressed in this discussion because they reflect the interplay between the Abiding and the Changing in human history, and this interplay is a fundamental aspect of the Islamic worldview. This worldview integrates the daily dynamic of human experience with the infinite resources of Divine Revelation.

The first important topic that must be addressed is the Arabic language itself. It is impossible to gain an accurate understanding of the Islamic perspective of reality while laboring under assumptions based on the socio- and religio-linguistic historical traditions of the *kufur* East and *kufur* West. The Islamic perspective of reality does not lend itself to any comparisons based on assumptions of the historical limitations and contingencies of non-Arabic languages. This is key to understanding the role of the **Generous Qur'an** in Islamic belief and *praxis*, which has focused on the ahistorical transcendence of the Arabic language.

After gaining a basic familiarity with the Islamic perspective of the uniqueness of the Arabic language, the reader is introduced to a contextual discussion of the **Generous Qur'an**. Again, it is essential to emphasize the unique and abiding importance of the **Generous Qur'an's** role in Islam, which non-Muslim readers may not be fully prepared to understand. The Islamic view is based upon the fact that the **Generous Qur'an** is the unaltered, ahistorical Word of **ALLAH** (*subhanahu wa ta'ala*). The epistemology of Islam stems from this basic

22

Chapter I. The Generous Qur'an: Light, Jewels and Pearls

fact, given the presence of *a priori* knowledge imbedded in the human essence as well as the essential role of our beloved Arabian **Prophet Muhammad** (*prayers and peace of* **ALLAH** *be upon him*), the World-Light-Splendor and the **Generous Qur'an** in *praxis*, in the decodification of this divine Word. The focus will be microscopically on the **Generous Qur'an**, *pari passu*, the Word of **ALLAH** (*subhanahu wa ta'ala*).

At that juncture, it will be imperative to concentrate on how Islamic reality is the abiding force of history. The **Generous Qur'an** is the only authentic Word of **ALLAH** (*subhanahu wa ta'ala*). Just imagination that the creation itself is words. The trajectory of being comes to confirm these words. One aspect of the inimitability of the Generous Qur'an is its simultaneous and complete relevance to both universal and particular aspects of the human condition as well as the entire universe. This means that revelation and human reason must play a complementary role. The *sine qua non* of the entire spectrum of this question is the authenticity of the divine revelation in the **Generous Qur'an**. There will be kaleidoscopic focus on the fact that only Islam provides the means for this complementary and balanced relationship, while historically the self-styled Christian and self-styled Jewish traditions never achieved a balance between the extremes of an intellectual, spiritual or political arrogance and a paralyzed fatalism, void of any real religious value and practice. This is because they are governed by dualistic ethics in which the people anesthetize themselves with "Thou shalt not kill" on Saturday or Sunday, while from Monday to Friday the social system practices a *de facto* war of all against all. Let the people of the Gospel govern by the Gospel, and let the people of the Torah govern by the Torah.

At this point, the research throws further light on these issues by addressing the relevance of the **Generous Qur'an** both within and

Chapter I. The Generous Qur'an: Light, Jewels and Pearls

beyond the context of the Muslim *ummah* (community). The Islamic ethos of approach to the **Generous Qur'an** is put in the context of the variety of human degrees of preparedness for understanding. Despite the fundamental importance of knowing the Arabic language for access to the authentic divine Word as represented in the **Generous Qur'an**, there are other, deeper prerequisites for finding guidance in it which are rooted in the fundamental conditions and stages of human consciousness. It is emphasized that the **Generous Qur'an** is for all humanity, and beyond.

Finally, the exposé addresses an Islamic "paradigm" for belief on the basis of a recognition and unification of the seen and unseen realms. These are integrated into the fundamental oneness (*tawhid*) of Islam through which the limits of historical, chronological vision are transcended. This process is a result of the *praxis* of the five daily Islamic prayers (*salaat*), which prepare the individual to embody the principle of *tawhid* in every aspect of life.

In conclusion, this book represents an attempt at articulating the already well-defined "paradigm" for understanding certain depths of Islamic belief and *praxis*, based upon an introduction to various requisites of an understanding of the **Generous Qur'an**. It is hoped that the reader will take this sincere intention and effort into consideration and let him or herself be engaged with an open heart in the pages that follow. *Insha'***ALLAH** (*subhanahu wa ta'ala*), God-Willing, the Lord will lead His dedicated servants to His Way. This is no more than an invitation and a call to Islam, the only way acceptable to **ALLAH** (*subhanahu wa ta'ala*).

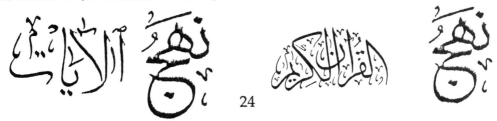

24

Chapter I. The Generous Qur'an: Light, Jewels and Pearls

Endnotes

[1]Jack C. Plano, et al., *Political Science Dictionary*, (Hinsdale, Illinois: The Dryden Press, 1973), p. 270.

[2]Thomas S. Kuhn, *The Structure of Scientific Revolutions*, (Chicago: University of Chicago Press, 1970), pp. 123-210.

N.B. The **Qur'anic** Arabic verses and English interpretation of the **Generous Qur'an**, cited in this Chapter and throughout the text of each following chapter, were taken from *The Meaning of the Glorious Qur'an: Text and Explanatory Translation, by Muhammad M. Pickthall*, (Mecca Al-Mukarramah (Saudi Arabia): Muslim World League-Rabita, 1977). For the sake of objectivity, we followed the text exactly.

25

CHAPTER II

The Uniqueness of the Arabic Language: A Historical and Linguistic Perspective

****

SURAH XII (12) *Joseph*

In the name of Allah, the Beneficent,
the Merciful.

1. Alif. Lam. Ra. These are verses of
the Scripture that maketh plain.

2. Lo! We have revealed it, a Lecture
in Arabic, that ye may understand.

بِسْمِ اللهِ الرَّحْمٰنِ الرَّحِيْمِ

الٓرٰ تِلْكَ اٰيٰتُ الْكِتٰبِ الْمُبِيْنِۚ

اِنَّآ اَنْزَلْنٰهُ قُرْاٰنًا عَرَبِيًّا لَّعَلَّكُمْ تَعْقِلُوْنَ

XII *Surah Yusuf,* **The Generous Qur'an** 12:1-2

****

In any endeavor to write about Islam and its relevance to
society, it is imperative to use the original Arabic terminology of the
Generous Qur'an, as well as Islamic scholarly methodology, to
convey original concepts as **ALLAH** (*subhanahu wa ta'ala*)
eloquently expressed them. English translations of the **Generous
Qur'an**, and indeed any translations into another language, are not

26

Chapter II. The Uniqueness of the Arabic Language

sufficient for this discussion because the universal and absolute meanings of the Divine Word have already been reduced and sifted out through the process of the translator's choice of words. For this reason, the authors have presented the major conceptual terminology of the discussion, as well as the **Generous Qur'anic** verses, in the original Arabic language. Because the **Generous Qur'an** is the only authentic, absolute and inimitable Word of **ALLAH** (*subhanahu wa ta'ala*), the meanings of the Arabic terms extend beyond any human's ability to narrow them down to a single definition. The glossary of terms at the beginning of this book, and the English interpretations we express in these pages, are only intended to give the reader a notion of the meanings in Arabic. Because of the infinity of meanings in the **Generous Qur'an**, the metaphors of Light, jewels and pearls have been used to give an idea of its transcendent beauty.

Because of the extensive use of Arabic in this volume and others, it is necessary to introduce the reader to some of the unique characteristics of the Arabic language. The reader should gain an appreciation for the fluidity, breadth, precision and flexibility of Arabic. These and many other unique qualities render it totally different from other languages in that it transcends the limitations of time which lead other languages into decay.

This chapter on linguistics is presented as a prelude to the following chapter on the **Generous Qur'an**. In the present chapter, we will discuss the historical limitations of non-Arabic languages. This will be followed by an explanation of how Arabic is itself ahistorical and not subject to the various changes, transformations and eliminations that have arisen through the interactions of non-Arabic languages with each other. It will be shown that the Arabic

27

language has been dominant in its contact with other languages and was able to survive intact through the march of history. Most importantly, its survival is a function of the commitment of **ALLAH** (*subhanahu wa ta'ala*) to preserve the **Generous Qur'an** and thereby the Arabic language, in its totality, from the time it was known to the world on through eternity. Arabic is the only language which transcends the entropic forces of history and thus becomes a negentropic force of reality.

Historical Limitations of Non-Arabic Languages

The traditional study of languages has been basically approached from two points of view. One approach, called historical linguistics, emphasizes the *diachronic* aspects of the changes in a language through time. The other approach, called descriptive linguistics, looks merely at the *synchronic* aspect, meaning that one disregards time as a factor and merely studies each stage of a language as having independent status. Ferdinand De Saussure (in 1916) was the first linguist to note this distinction in his assertion that changes occur as a succession of synchronic states in a fortuitous fashion. Others believed that changes were more systematic. However, by studying successive stages in synchronic grammar, the historical linguist can trace the historical development of a language.[1]

Regardless of the scholastic assertion that language develops in a series of successive stages, most languages are perceived to change through time in a continuous fashion. The problem, however, is that linguists are unable to study language development as a

Chapter II. The Uniqueness of the Arabic Language

flowing process because they are limited by a methodology which only permits them to study *ex post facto* stages of languages. They can do no more than study abstractions from the observable reality. Furthermore, the situational use of language that they study is affected by differences in the speakers' geographical location and social class, as well as the degree of observed formality. The analyst thus may idealize his data somewhat to compensate for his lack of complete knowledge or direct evidence for the multiplicity of possible linguistic variations.[2]

Linguists have also asserted that language is perpetuated and changed through the processes of language acquisition, in which each new generation of speakers adds its own variations to the language as time goes on. The changes that accrue in some languages are not necessarily the product of imperfect learning but rather have their own persistence and direction. This is complicated by the fact that certain social stigmas may encourage individuals to be careful to avoid speaking in the slang of their original culture. In general, however, historical language change is a product of forces beyond the individual level.

Language specialists have generally felt that a meaningful study of language change should span about four or five centuries. Over this length of time, systematic, large-scale and dramatic changes become more apparent, while nevertheless one is still observing the same language. In summary, linguists have traditionally taken two approaches to the study of language change. First, they study the different isolated principles, structures and grammar of completed changes, and, secondly, they study the processes of change as it relates to socio-linguistic influences.

As a striking example of such change, if one looks at forms of

29

the Lord's Prayer (found in the Bible and read by many Christians) that were written at different times, one can see the numerous changes in spelling and terminology that have occurred over time. The alteration of the Bible in such an arbitrary manner is testimony to its susceptibility and vulnerability to historical time changes. Thus, the original Biblical wording is not held sacred nor is it immune from arbitrary change. In fact, there is nothing in existence today which actually represents the "original wording". This presents very serious repercussions for the strength of the Christians' belief in the so-called "Word" of God.

The Lord's Prayer

Authorized version (1611)
Our father which art in heauen, hallowed be thy name. Thy kyngdome come. Thy will be done in earth, as it is in heauen. Giue vs this day our daily bread. And forgiue vs our debts, as we forgiue our debters. And lead vs not into temptation, but deliuer vs from euill.

Wycliff's version (late fourteenth century)
Oure fadir þat art in heuenes, halwid be þi name; þi reume or kyngdom come to þe. Be þi wille don in herþe as it is doun in heuene. ȝeue to vs to-day oure eche dayes bred. And forȝeue to vs oure dettis, þat is oure synnys, as we forȝeuen tu oure dettouris, þat is to men þat han synned in vs. And lede vs not in-to temptacion, but delyuere vs from euyl.

30

Chapter II. The Uniqueness of the Arabic Language

Old English (West Saxon, ca. 1000)
Fæder ure þu þe eart on heofonum, si þin nama gehalgod; to-
becume þin rice; gewurþe þin willa on eorðan swa swa on
heofonum; urne gedæghwamlican hlaf syle us to dæg; and forgyf us
ure gyltas, swa swa we forgyfað urum gyltendum; and ne gelæd þu
us on costnunge, ac alys us of yfele.

Modern German
Unser Vater in dem Himmel. Nein Name werde geheiligt.
Dein Reich komme. Dein Wille geschehe auf Erden wie im
Himmel. Unser täglich Brot gib uns heute. Und vergib uns unsere
Schulden, wie wir unsern Schuldigern vergeben. Und führe uns
nict in Versuchung, sondern erlöse uns von dem Übel.

Old High German (East Frankish, Tatian's version, ca. 830)
Fater unser thu thar bist in himile, si giheilagot thin namo,
queme thin rihhi, si thin uuillo, so her in himile ist so si her in
erdu; unsar brot tagalihhaz gib uns hiutu, inti furlaz uns unsara
sculdi, so uuir furlazemes unsaren sculdigon; inti ni gileitest unsih
in costunga, uzouh arlose unsih fon ubile.

Welsh (standard version, sixteenth century)
Ein tad, yr hwn wyt yn y nefoedd: sancteiddier dy enw. Deled
dy deyrnas. Gwneler dy ewyllys, megis yn y nef, felly ar y ddaear
hefyd. Dyro i ni heddiw ein bara beunyddiol. A maddau i ni ein
dyledion, fel y maddeuwn ninnau i'n dyledwyr. Ac nac arwain ni i
brofedigaeth, eithr gwared ne rhag drwg.

Chapter II. The Uniqueness of the Arabic Language

Hungarian

Mi Atyank, ki vagy a mennyekben, szenteltessék meg a te neved; jöjjön el a te országod; legyen meg a te akaratod, mint a mennyben ugy a földön is. A mi mindennapi kenyerünket add meg nekünk ma. És bocsásd meg a mi vétkeinket, miképen mi is megbocsátunk azoknak, a kik ellenünk vétkeztek; és ne vígy minket kísértetbe, de szabadíts meg minket a gonosztól.[3]

The *Surah Al-Fatihah*, the first *Surah* of the **Generous Qur'an**, however, is recited by all Muslims in precisely the same words, and has never been modified or altered in any way. The Arabic language manifests the opposite of the non-Arabic tendency to modify texts over time. It thus solves the problem of historical language change. *Surah Al-Fatihah* is presented in full on the following page.

32

****

SURAH I (1) *The Opening*

1. In the name of Allah the Beneficent, the Merciful.

بِسْمِ اللهِ الرَّحْمٰنِ الرَّحِيْمِ ۝

2. Praise be to Allah, Lord of the Worlds:

اَلْحَمْدُ لِلّٰهِ رَبِّ الْعٰلَمِيْنَ ۝

3. The Beneficent, the Merciful:

الرَّحْمٰنِ الرَّحِيْمِ ۝

4. Owner of the Day of Judgement.

مٰلِكِ يَوْمِ الدِّيْنِ ۝

5. Thee (alone) we worship; Thee (alone) we ask for help.

اِيَّاكَ نَعْبُدُ وَاِيَّاكَ نَسْتَعِيْنُ ۝

6. Show us the straight path:

اِهْدِنَا الصِّرَاطَ الْمُسْتَقِيْمَ ۝

7. The path of those whom Thou hast favoured; Not (the path) of those who earn Thine anger nor of those who go astray.

صِرَاطَ الَّذِيْنَ اَنْعَمْتَ عَلَيْهِمْ غَيْرِ الْمَغْضُوْبِ عَلَيْهِمْ وَلَا الضَّآلِّيْنَ ۝

I *Surah Al-Fatihah*, **The Generous Qur'an** 1:1-7

****

33

Chapter II. The Uniqueness of the Arabic Language

While the general topic of language change is pertinent to the study of most languages, the Arabic language is different. It presents a totally new classification which transcends historical analysis due to its timeless applicability. The methodology of all man-made paradigms of language change studies does not apply to Arabic. The Arabic language is the oldest popular, immune, autonomous, homeostatic, standard, isomorphic, integrated, holy and holistic language in use in the world. It is a "time-language" and a "language in time". Many languages of the world come and go, each changing dramatically through the march of history. None of them were here to stay except the Arabic language, because the latter is the language in which **ALLAH** (*subhanahu wa ta'ala*) chose to articulate reality and which therefore governs the multiplicity of circumstances in the human condition, in all of its sectors, including science, technology, epistemology and other realms of learning. Arabic can only be understood and conceptualized through its *own* empirical rules, grammar, syntax, phonology and other concepts of social and historical linguistics. Arabic has its own *modus operandi* for its *modus vivendi,* regardless of what epoch of history or what location in which one lives.[4]

Social and economic variables of any *kufur* society influence the structural formation of its language. Through time, the social conditions change and therefore the conceptions and meanings of the terms in non-Arabic languages change. As a result, it is difficult for any *kufur* non-Arabic scholar who has graduated with an M.A. or a Ph.D. in a particular field in English or French, for example, to understand with ease a book which was written in his own language 400 or 500 years ago. Meanings change through time, terms change from place to place and it is difficult to put oneself in

34

the frame of mind of intellectuals who lived 500 years ago.[5] The English language has changed dramatically in the last 400 to 500 years. A person has to study six to ten years in order to understand the conceptual meaning of certain literature written in any particular era. This is true for every language in history except the authentic Arabic language.

The question becomes why the English language and other non-Arabic languages do not survive and keep their autonomy through the march of history, while the sacred and immune Arabic language, on the contrary, has kept its autonomy and conceptual meaning in all realms. These realms include science, mathematics, medicine, technology, physics, telepathy, astrogeophysics, nuclear physics, astronomy, chemistry and others. It is imperative to understand that non-Arabic languages such as English, French and German, etc., are "historical" languages and thereby they live and have meaning only within the framework of each particular epoch of history. These languages do not transcend their contemporaneous meanings in any absolute sense because they are not the carriers of the Word of **ALLAH** (*subhanahu wa ta'ala*), and therefore they lack an authentic and absolute frame of reference. Thus, each author redefines his local reality and the order of things based upon his cultural, professional, and ideational conceptions, which are encapsulated within the illusionary interplay between space and time. Each *kufur* writer has a local and contemporaneous reality which he articulates in certain words and concepts that are partially compatible with his epoch.[6] The lack of an authentic, absolute frame of reference which is based on a universal perception has made every language other than Arabic a prisoner of its time. From this perspective, the Arabic language is not like any

35

Chapter II. The Uniqueness of the Arabic Language

other language. Every other language is historically bound, while Arabic is an ahistorical language. That is to say, it is a language that transcends every epoch of history. It is compatible with and accountable to every epoch.

It is easy for any person who has a simple working knowledge of the Arabic language to read and understand any Arabic book, regardless of the time dimension in which the book was written. A person with less than a high school education could read a book written in Arabic one thousand years ago and understand it with ease. From the Islamic perspective, the terms in Arabic have kept their conceptual and empirical meaning throughout history because of their authentic frame of reference in the **Generous Qur'an,** which is the actual Word of **ALLAH** (*subhanahu wa ta'ala*). The meanings of the terms are associated with the timeless applicability of the all-encompassing divine perception. The **Generous Qur'an** in itself is not man-made; it is divinely ordained. God-consciousness transcends the particular to aspire to the universal. **ALLAH** (*subhanahu wa ta'ala*) is the First and the Last, and therefore His Word becomes timeless: beyond time yet compatible with every epoch of history. Its Light, pearls and jewels are forever glowing and gleaming.

Every language is the manifestation as well as the externality of human beings in a social context. Every human society has developed a medium for communication. This medium, in its style of articulation and structural formation, as well as grammatical standards, constitutes the living language of that society. The human being is, from his inception, a system that absorbs the norms and the sounds of his local environment. The individual is, in part, a function of his social system and thus grows

36

up to be at home in the language of his local environment. The language and the social system usually live only for a certain span of time. The individual's lifespan is usually shorter than that of his social environment, including social norms and language itself.

The social system is a dynamic system, not a static one. Therefore most languages are in a state of constant evolution.[7] The evolution of a language *transcends* only one or two epochs of history and as a result, through the passage of time, a language is born, lives and then dies. A new language then establishes its legitimacy by becoming prominent in its structural, syntactic, morphological, semantic and phonological application. Through time this language will be the medium of the working condition of the society. It will achieve its heyday and its peak, but ultimately, as a result of the forces of *entropy*, it will decline and slowly wither away. The language and its people, as well as the social structure which encompassed both, will eventually disappear. This is not the case, however, with the Arabic language. All historical languages except Arabic follow the blueprint of this chronology. It is well known that many languages have existed in history of which there is either no trace, or else such traces that exist are difficult to decipher and understand. Such languages can never be fully reconstructed and recovered. Many of them are lost forever.

The Arabic Language as an Ahistorical Language

The Arabic language is the only living language which has kept its autonomy and structural, paradigmatic and isomorphic formation through time. It is thus an ahistorical language.

The Arabic, Qur'anic and Islamic Paradigm:
Light, Jewels and Pearls

Chapter II. The Uniqueness of the Arabic Language

It is imperative to understand that the Arabic language is not like any other language in the world, because of the fact that it transcends the contemporaneous limitations of any particular epoch of history. *Kufur* linguistic analysts and scholars are consciously or unconsciously misrepresenting the Arabic language in their attempts to categorize Arabic on the same level with other, extinct languages and/or their reconstructed prototypes. Dead languages and reconstructed languages cannot be compared with Arabic because Arabic is still alive and it will continue to live with its own historically unique autonomy throughout eternity. Therefore, the Arabic language has a unique qualitative and quantitative dimension which makes it incommensurable with any other, historical, dead or living languages. The reconstruction of an extinct language through a hypothetical quantitative method faces irreconcilable methodological adversities.[8] Nevertheless, the reconstruction and quantification of languages in general does play an auxiliary role.

"This means that there is no necessary correlation between language type and historical origin, so that shared typological features can neither be taken as excluding nor as indicating geneological relationship. Attempts to use isomorphism of structure either as a short cut to geneological classification (as has sometimes been done in the past for instance in the field of Bantu and American Indian linguistics) or as a way of penetrating further into the prehistory of a language than can be achieved by means of reconstruction are therefore quite without justification. However convenient such solutions might appear in theory, the historical linguist has to admit that for the time being, at least, the only proven means of reaching beyond attested language states remains systematic reconstruction."[9]

The geneological origins as well as the prototypes of the Arabic language become irrelevant when it is considered that the Arabic language has survived through the march of history. Many languages have existed in history which became uprooted, with no trace of their autonomy. Just as science cannot bring a dead person back to life, any sociolinguist or vocational linguist who is concentrating on reconstructing an irrecoverable language will face a deadlock.

Because the Arabic language is alive, it cannot be defined according to other semitic languages, which are mostly dead. While the latter are lost forever as popular, lively languages, the Arabic language on the contrary will survive forever. The structural paradigmatic formation of these other languages constitutes a changing variable of history. All languages other than Arabic can be shown to change dramatically over the years. Therefore, they cannot become the medium to transcend history. Because other languages cannot go back and forth in history, they are prisoners of history. Only the Arabic language can march forward and backward in history, due to its timeless dimension. Thus, any conscious person who wants to know about the breadth of a given subject-matter can find refuge in the Arabic language. Through the Arabic language, one may explore many empirical dimensions of applied research. Hypothetically speaking, a person wanting to know about the empirical reality that existed one thousand years ago in any area of the world might not find an authentic primary source that could describe the issue under focus. In the absence of authentic historical sources, he will turn to the secondary intellectual deliberation of those scholars of his century who have constructed hypotheses on that issue. These hypothetical sources, though they may have been written with good intentions and been widely admired, have, through the passage of time, proven to be limited in explaining the contextual dimensions of historical reality.[10] In many cases, a scholar would be fortunate to find more than one or two sources about an issue existing in a society a thousand years ago, because few societies have ever kept a continuous record of events over a thousand year period. In fact, few societies ever existed for over a thousand years. Even if one did exist, no one scholar or group of scholars is able to understand *in toto* the lexicon, the analytical tools or the conceptual frame of mind of that society. It is only the Arabic language which maintained its autonomy from time immemorial up to the present day. It therefore established its *de facto* empirical legitimacy in fulfilling the role of an authentic practical medium by which to transcend, yet encompass history.

The linguistic structural formation indicates that Arabic is not governed by history or by time. Other languages such as English, French or Russian are linguistically structured to be the prisoner of history and time because their conception of time is unilinear. Therefore their linguistic structural formation is typologized by a three-part time conception: the past, the present and the future. An analyst who wants to write about any relevant issue becomes a prisoner of his epoch of history and his time dimension. Therefore, his vision becomes encapsulated by the illusionary interplay between space and time. An analyst can only dissect any issue within a time frame; he cannot extend his analysis to a timeless

40

Chapter II. The Uniqueness of the Arabic Language

contextual dimension. The encapsulated *kufur* analyst must profess that he cannot understand *in toto* the historical background of the issue. Neither could he give us definite guidelines for the future. The only thing he can confidently say is that the issue under focus is in motion and thereby his speculations are no more than hypothetical personifications which become the changing, ultimately irrelevant variables of history. One of the major reasons for this is that the medium in which he is expressing himself is a language which is a prisoner of history. The second reason is that his vision and intrinsic values have been manipulated, truncated and kidnapped by *kufur* social inculcation.

Each sentence in English or French must have a verb that functions according to a time frame. That is to say it has a beginning, a life span, and an end. This gives it a unilinear direction, whereas Arabic is a time-free, holy, holistic language. It is very well known that in Arabic not every sentence must have a verb. Those sentences without a verb are called "noun sentences"; those with a verb are called "verb sentences". This is one indicator that time does not govern Arabic linguistic articulation. It is very easy in Arabic to speak of a sentence which is indicative of a present situation, yet refers to the future ex-post-history in terms of witnessing it in one's own present time.[11] One sentence can easily travel back and forth through time because the concept of time and space does not apply of necessity to Arabic. Therefore, the thought patterns, the vision and the profound linguistic articulation become also timeless. It is easy in Arabic to speak of an Absolute God Who is the First and the Last. This "timeless" meaning conceptually indicates no beginning and no end. Therefore, with that frame of reference in mind, the span of time which is labelled as history

41

becomes no more than an illusion. Therefore, the Arabic language is the only language which can host the Absolute. If it can host the Absolute, then it can travel through history and encompass history.[12]

So any person who wants to know about any issue or science (including in the sub-atomic realm) whether it was in the past or will be in the future, has to read, with guidance from **ALLAH** (*subhanahu wa ta'ala*). the only alive and authentic book of the Absolute. One can say, therefore, without any reservation, that the Arabic language stands out in history as the only language which articulates, forecasts and predicts reality as it is indicated in the **Generous Qur'an**. It has crystalized itself as an autonomous, unique language throughout the Spaceship Earth which has established its own apparati and standards. In addition, its flexibility and dynamism has allowed the appearance of different dialects to interact within the Arabic language producing "diglossic" communities. However, the presence of various dialects is a blessing from **ALLAH** (*subhanahu wa ta'ala*) which registers human differences but which can never cancel out the formal, classical Arabic. This is because all of the Arabic dialects have one frame of reference, the **Generous Qur'an**, which is "generous" with many dialects and readings, and which standardizes the language and makes it sovereign. The **Generous Qur'an** in itself is sovereign. Therefore, the medium of its expression becomes sovereign, pure, immune and inimitable.

"Beautiful writing increases the truth in clarity,"

Muhakkak

42

The Metamorphosis Into Arabic

It is next to impossible to think in abstract terms dissected from the multiplicity of empirical reality. The Islamic use of the Arabic language constituted an abiding force of history. It has spread through many parts of the world and it has survived through the march of history. The transmission and survival of Arabic intact means historically that this language has unique characteristics which are beyond rational deliberation.

One of the main characteristics of the Arabic language is its dynamic ability to handle profoundly and eloquently not only conflict resolution but conflict management. Any student who understands the dimensions of historical linguistics asserts that language is not a product of a year or two but it is a culmination of many epochs of cultural integration and metamorphosis. The survival of any particular language implies that that language has overcome many confrontations, indicating an inherent dynamism which helped it to surmount all types of tribulation.[13] No culture in the world negotiates willingly to change its value system, its language, its norms, its expectations and its concepts of good and bad overnight. Every society has faced turbulence from within and without. The result of these confrontations will ultimately end (in ex-post-history) in the establishment of the Straight Way that can never be uprooted if it represents authentic reality based on the science of *tawhid*.(Oneness). Truth is auto-legitimating and its is not in need of either sci-tech, hi-tech, SDI (Strategic Defense Initiative), ISDN (Integrated Services Digital Network) or neuro-technology to establish it. A conqueror or a power-monger may manipulate a political system for a few decades, but soon he will be

43

as if he never was. The Arabic language was able to play a role in
history because of its embedded dynamism in conflict management
of culture as well as conflict resolution.

When the Arabs, as carriers of the messianic mission, called
the hearts of the Egyptians to the Absolute, the pre-Islamic
Egyptians responded to this call to **ALLAH** (*subhanahu wa ta'ala*)
and made submission as Muslims. The iron law of Arabic
dynamism is imbedded in the message in its absolute, irrevocable
and unequivocal dimension. At the primordial stages when any
individual makes submission in Islam, he mysteriously goes
through a metamorphosis which redefines his or her self, his or her
sense of loyalty and identity, and his or her sense of community.
The Arabic language was able to penetrate the apparent and the
hidden dimension of culture to redefine an individual in terms of
the dictates of *tawhid* as delineated in the **Generous Qur'an** in the
Arabic language. There is no question that most non-Arab peoples
who make submission to **ALLAH** (*subhanahu wa ta'ala*) in Islam
will think and speak in their historically extinct language for a time.
However, through time they will rectify themselves to the Straight
Path to become the embodiment of the authentic word of **ALLAH**
(*subhanahu wa ta'ala*) as it is articulated in the **Generous Qur'an** in
Arabic, which becomes their frame of reference. Thereby, the word
becomes the living *praxis* which will be transmitted to the next
generation. The Arabic language was able to perform a therapeutic
function for those newcomers coming home in the primordial
stages of contact, and elevate them to the real world of the beyond,
not the world of make-believe.

The Arabic language was historically able to become a "conflict
manager" among the conglomeration of cultures. It did not degrade

44

the already existing culture and language, nor try to abolish it. Rather it managed it in such a way as to make the transformation to Arabic delicate and profound. The Egyptians, for example, in the early days of acceptance of Islam kept their language, their habits and their cultures. But when they made full submission to **ALLAH** (*subhanahu wa ta'ala*) and became Muslims, the Arabic language was able to slowly penetrate and re-define their values and goals as well as to strip them (at all levels of the stratification) of their pre-Islamic language which eventually became extinct. The Arabic language eventually took precedence over any other language. Through that transformation however, the dynamic, lively and gregarious personality of the Egyptians was expressed through the Arabic language in the creation of a particular dialect.[14]

Anyone who has knowledge of the Arabic language realizes that it is flexible and adaptable. As a result, individuals or whole communities having whatever personalities or style of articulation will find a refuge in the Arabic language because it allows them to express their particular unique individualism while allowing them to unite with the universal.

Historical Language Contact

Any student of historical linguistics is familiar with the effect of the contact between languages. It is usually the case that the transfer of language materials across language boundaries is carried out by certain bilingual individuals. It has been a well-established pattern that the precise nature and extent of linguistic exchange is contingent upon the detailed circumstances of social and cultural

45

Chapter II. The Uniqueness of the Arabic Language

relations between the communities concerned. The crux of this discussion is the notion of contact which should be understood from the perspective of close geographical proximity as well as trade relations. When cultures with different degrees of sophistication encounter each other, the culture which is predominant will influence the one which is less dominant. It is usually the case that trade relations between producers or conveyors of certain commodities will influence the clientele to adopt the exporters' terminology regarding the names of some of these commodities. The student of historical linguistics is familiar with this phenomenon because it has been a well-documented, acceptable and respected fact of recent language history. Popular names of particular objects of international trade such as cotton, coffee, tea or tobacco, have historically travelled with the conveyors, and through time have become part of the consumer language. For nations which are fully bicultural, not only the lexicon of the two languages will be shared but also phonological aspects and grammatical rules. The lexicon, however, reflects the culture of its speakers more than the other aspects.

The Germanic peoples borrowed much of their lexicon from the Christian Church and classical antiquity. During the early period of contact, a great deal of terminology came partially from both the classical and vernacular Latin. Approximately 500 or so words of the Germanic peoples originated from this early contact. Such words are considered to be borrowed because they share a similar relationship to the Latin. Those aspects of the Germanic cultures which were most influenced by Roman (Latin speaking) culture share the most similar lexicon in such fields as horticulture, building in stone, book-learning, the Church, technical skills and others.

An example of the borrowed lexicon is found in the Latin word *cappa* which was *kappa* in Old High German and is *kappe* in Modern German (and *cap* in English). The Latin word *schola* was *scuola* in Old High German and *schule* in Modern German (meaning school in English), etc. Once a word is borrowed it becomes an indigenous part of the lexicon as if it were a native word. It thenceforth can be affected by the society and culture in the same manner as other terminology.

In addition to relation through historical contact, Latin is geneologically related to English and German. For example, one finds certain consistencies between cognate words in Latin that use the letter *p*, and words using the letter *f* in German. Other examples include the use of the letter *t* in Latin which corresponds to the letter *d* in German (*tres* in Latin is *drei* in German). The is because Germanic language underwent the first consonant shift whereas Latin kept the Proto-Indo-European consonants. Languages may then come into contact with one another at different time periods. They may go through a series of corresponding changes and experience an extended relationship including contact at more than one point in history.

The English language also derived much of its lexicon, morphs and word patterns from Latin and French at different periods of time. Many new scientific terms have come out of this contact with Latin, such as *insecticide, binoculars, supersonic* and *carboniferous*. To trace the origin of various words, one reconstructs backwards until he finds a comparable form in the donor language. However, comparisons relating to ancient borrowings are often difficult to directly observe. Some words become fully assimilated into the

47

English system, losing their "foreign" or alien phonology. These borrowed words thereby come to be pronounced in ways which are identical with those of native English words, like *garage* and *restaurant*, which derived from French but which are pronounced differently in English. Other words are more incompletely integrated. In some cases, there are detectable similarities in the synchronic phonology of the recipient language. In other cases the phonological structure is considerable different and a borrowed word will go undetected. This occurs when an adapted intermediary form of the word (not its original form) is borrowed. For example, the Indian and Pakistani languages have borrowed many English words through the medium of "Indian English".

Loan-words, or borrowed words, must also be adapted to the syntactical rules of the recipient language by behaving in the common framework when constructing plurals or inflecting for the present tense and for the past tense as well. Some nouns, however, retained their original plural morphs from the donor language such as with Latin words like *criterion*, *criteria* and *phenomenon*, *phenomena*. Most borrowed words in English, however, follow without exception the productive morphological rules in English.

Historically, the Christian religion was transmitted to pagan peoples linguistically as well as metaphysically. Many of the Christian concepts were passed on in the original Latin form such as *papa*, which became *pope* in English and *Papst* in Modern German, and *monasterium* in Latin which became *minister* in English and *Muenster* in German. Also, *altare* in Latin became *altar* in English. Other English words related to Christian phenomena were translated or adapted to English to become a more familiar linguistic form. In some cases a new construct was created and

48

modeled on the foreign source where the constituent elements and grammatical rules followed the native pattern. Some examples of this are the Latin word *euangelista* which was translated into *evangelist, paganus* into *pagan, resurrectio* into *resurrection, spiritus sanctus* into *Holy Ghost, trinitas* into *trinity, misericordia* into *mercy, ascensio* into *ascension* and *euangelium* into *gospel*.[15]

This form of translation of lexicon was an appealing solution for the foreign recipients, for it helped to localize and internalize the concepts into their own perspective of reality consistent with their own linguistic structure.

Aside from translating or adapting borrowed words, there is another approach called semantic extension which refers to the way a foreign concept may be taken into a language. In this case the semantic range of a term with a similar meaning in the native vocabulary is expanded to include the new meaning of the foreign word. Germanic words like *God, Heaven, Hell* and *evil* are examples of this semantic extension. From their original reference to limited non-Christian phenomena, these same words were then used to accommodate the broader meanings inherent in the Christian framework. The word *God*, which is common to all the Germanic languages, does not appear to have any linkages with the Latin *deus* or the Greek *theos*. It is not the word used by the prophets, nor is it the actual name that **ALLAH** (*subhanahu wa ta'ala*) uses to refer to Himself. The term *God* is referred to, in the oldest records available, as having neuter gender which suggests to analysts that it may have originally been an adjective referring to something which is "invoked".[16]

In the history of languages there is not one language which kept its autonomy through the march of history. Languages affected

49

each other, in part, and borrowed from each other to the point that they became the changing and encapsulated variables of history which decayed and withered away through time. The only exception to that is the Arabic language. Arabic, therefore, is the only transcendental language. Thereby, linguistic theorists may apply their theories and paradigms to Germanic, Indo-European, African and Asian, etc., languages, but they do not dare apply them to the Arabic language. If they would, they would become overwhelmed by the uniqueness of Arabic, which transcends their theoretical approaches and revolutionizes their rational deliberations. Those, if there are any, who insist on trying to apply their *kufur* linguistic paradigms to the study of Arabic are wasting their time. Arabic is unique and incommensurate with any such paradigms because **ALLAH** (*subhanahu wa ta'ala*) chose it to articulate His reality which is transcendental through time and becomes a living being: a Time Being and a Being in Time.

The Transcendence of the Arabic Language

When "objective" scholars look at the unique, unprecedented historical phenomena of how the Arabic language came into contact with other languages, there are two epochs which must be distinguished: that of the Arabic language prior to carrying the mission and transmission of Islam and that of the Arab language afterwards. It must be remembered that the Arabs used to be great traders prior to Islam. When they were traders, they carried with them their commodities. They used to send a caravan in the winter and one in the summer, and at other times when needed. They

50

went to a Syrian city called Tedmur which used to be the central market (or *suq*) for caravans from around the region. During the pre-Islamic era, when the Arabs from the Arabian Peninsula went to the northern areas, they brought only their commodities and exchanged what they needed. These Arabs did not convey any influence other than a few terms related to their merchandise. The culture of the Roman Empire in Syria, therefore, kept its autonomy. The same applied to the cultures of the early Persian Empire and pre-Islamic Egypt.[17]

The Arabs were extremely advanced prior to Islam in their linguistics and profound articulation of poetry. One poem could be a source of setting tribes against each other to point of war, or it could elevate the reputation of an unknown tribe to the top of the agenda of Arab affairs. The beautiful prolonged poetry which used to be hung on the walls of the *Ka'aba* in pre-Islamic days made it a central gathering place for poetry competitions and recitations.

Each tribe would also glorify its pagan gods which were fabricated out of different materials. As mentioned earlier, one tribe which had made its god out of dates found that in time of need and hunger there was no reluctance in eating this false god. While the Arabs were very sophisticated and intelligent, the pre-Islamic era was, nevertheless, called the "Days of Ignorance" because the Arabs were not yet the carriers of the messianic mission of *tawhid*. When they went to the north, they were not interested in anything except merchant dealings. The same applied to their commercial journeys and relations with the "advanced" cultures of the Romans and Persians to the north and east, and the Egyptians to the west.[18]

When **ALLAH** (*subhanahu wa ta'ala*) chose the Arabs as the carriers of the Islamic mission, the message became totally different.

51

Chapter II. The Uniqueness of the Arabic Language

Due to the fact that Islam is a unique religion in the world with a Book that is the actual, authentic Word of **ALLAH** (*subhanahu wa ta'ala*) and that articulates, to the final detail, the *modus operandi* and *modus vivendi* of a divinely ordained lifestyle, it became apparent that the Light of the World Splendor has no limitations. When the Muslim Arabs became the carriers of the message of *tawhid*, this means that they would have to speak the Word of **ALLAH** (*subhanahu wa ta'ala*) as it was authentically revealed. No one would dare to add or subtract one letter. The word *tawhid* means Oneness: Oneness of the Word, Oneness of the Book and Oneness of the Way. This is why Islam is the Only Way. When any issue arises among authentic Muslim Arabs, and authentic Muslims in general, their first step is to refer to what **ALLAH** (*subhanahu wa ta'ala*) said in the **Generous Qur'an,** not to human deliberation. The **Generous Qur'an** teaches us what needs to be done. It raises the questions, sets the methodology and gives us the answers so that individuals who follow the Word of **ALLAH** (*subhanahu wa ta'ala*) can become the embodiment of the Law in order to be on the Straight Path. No human cognition could ever duplicate the Word of **ALLAH** (*subhanahu wa ta'ala*) with all its infinite myriad of meanings in its profound, eloquent and radiant articulation. Therefore, when **ALLAH** (*subhanahu wa ta'ala*) (through the Muslim Arabs) opened the hearts of the northern, eastern, western and southern peoples, they were not giving them coffee, tea, cotton, Atari, computers, scientific technology or high technology. They were giving them a straight way of life and a divinely ordained value system which elevated them from darkness to light, from crookedness to straightness and from paganism to *tawhid* (Oneness).

Chapter II. The Uniqueness of the Arabic Language

Those in *kufur* societies whom **ALLAH** (*subhanahu wa ta'ala*) called to Islam and whose hearts and minds were opened by **ALLAH** (*subhanahu wa ta'ala*) began to radiate Light in their fiber and fabric. They came home to Islam. They were not "converted" to Islam; rather, they were rectified and directed to their real home base, which is Islam. When they got a glimpse of Islam and of the authenticity of the message of *tawhid* and the seriousness of why humans have been put on earth, everything else became secondary to them. Many of them raced to understand and to learn the authentic Word of **ALLAH** (*subhanahu wa ta'ala*) in Arabic, which is the **Generous Qur'an**. Their own language and ways started to become secondary to Islam.

What is more valuable in life than to learn the Word of **ALLAH** (*subhanahu wa ta'ala*) and the Science of *Tawhid*, as well as the *usul-al-din* (Islamic jurisprudence)? Every person must remember that it is **ALLAH** (*subhanahu wa ta'ala*) Who teaches people. When those whom **ALLAH** (*subhanahu wa ta'ala*) has called to Islam have manifested their ideational rectification, **ALLAH** (*subhanahu wa ta'ala*) gives them Light inwardly and outwardly. Many Islamic scholars have been non-Arabs. They learned Arabic in the anticipation of understanding and navigating in the infinite ocean of the Word of **ALLAH** (*subhanahu wa ta'ala*). The **Prophet Muhammad** (*prayers and peace of* **ALLAH** *be upon him*) said that any person who speaks Arabic is an Arab. The **Prophet Muhammad** (*prayers and peace of* **ALLAH** *be upon him*) himself was unlettered and could not read or write. He could not even recognize the shapes of the letters. Nevertheless, many scholars who came after him learned the Arabic lexicon, syntax and grammar, to become great scholars. One of the primary books of

53

Chapter II. The Uniqueness of the Arabic Language

Arabic grammar was written by an Indian scholar. Also the *hadith* collector, Imam Al-Bukhari, was originally from the Islamic state of Bukhara, which is now in the south of Russia. Abu Hamid Al-Ghazzali, who wrote volumes about *The Revival of Islamic Jurisprudence* and many other books in Arabic was originally from Persia. Islam is not a nationality. It transcends nationalism and it unites particulars with the universals under what is called *Al-Ubudiyyah* (total surrender and slavery to the Lord).

When the Muslim Arabs carried the language of the **Generous Qur'an** to those individuals whom **ALLAH** (*subhanahu wa ta'ala*) had called to Islam, the latter went through a process of metamorphosis. The uniqueness of that experience was that the Arabic language was able to perform a conflict management function. If one wants to learn **ALLAH's** (*subhanahu wa ta'ala*) Word, he has to learn it in Arabic. Even if he wants to buy and sell, he has to follow the *Shari'ah*. One needs, therefore, to learn what is *halal* and *haram* (permitted and forbidden). If one wants to marry, he or she has to follow the Islamic rules. When one wants to perform *salaat* (the five daily prayers), prior to that he must know what is ablution, including *tahara* and *ghusul*. There is a word or phrase which delineates every aspect of life.

In Islam, one cannot believe in certain values and practice something else. When one believes in the Word of **ALLAH** (*subhanahu wa ta'ala*), it becomes *praxis*. One then lives according to the Word of **ALLAH** (*subhanahu wa ta'ala*). If one wants to live according to the Word of **ALLAH** (*subhanahu wa ta'ala*) in Arabic, one has to learn how to understand it according to its own *modus operandi*, because Arabic is an ahistorical language. One can travel back and forth in the Arabic language without any difficulty. It is

54

Chapter II. The Uniqueness of the Arabic Language

the only living language, because **ALLAH** (*subhanahu wa ta'ala*) committed Himself to preserving the Word and preserving the Arabic language in which He chose to dramatize and crystalize His hidden and apparent power in the universe. The Arabic language is the only language that the Absolute (**ALLAH** (*subhanahu wa ta'ala*)) chose in which to convey His Message and preserve it. Thereby it came to be part of the conglomerous and rigorous, abiding and surviving forces of history, whereas all other languages constituted no more than the changing and collapsing forces of history.

The Arab-Islamic language navigated and cleansed the lifestyle and languages of the various cultures which came into contact with it. The dynamism of the Arab-Islamic language was able to survive because it was extremely sensitive to the conflict management of these people. This is because it penetrated every aspect of life and it was designed by **ALLAH** (*subhanahu wa ta'ala*) to be problem-solving and conflict managing for the human predicament in the anticipation of rectifying humanity to healthiness, openness and straightness. Because of this, some people learned Arabic and became Arabs while their own indigenous language was lost forever without recovery. Some of them even became the main carriers, conveyors, scholars and articulators of the Arabic language throughout the Arab world from the Atlantic to the Arabian-Islamic Gulf. Some of them kept their indigenous language while learning Arabic.

Thus the Arabic language became an infinite source of conceptions and words. Many other languages therefore borrowed from Arabic and it became the language of conduct in some non-Arab countries, such as in Africa, for example. Historically, the

Chapter II. The Uniqueness of the Arabic Language

Arabic language became the main scholarly and authentic reference for the Absolute, **ALLAH** (*subhanahu wa ta'ala*), and His domain.[19] It also became the frame of reference for the sciences. As previously mentioned, many scholars and students throughout the world went to many different Islamic educational centers to be educated in places like *Makkah Al-Mukarramah, Medina Al-Munawwirah,* Baghdad, Kufa, Damascus, Fez, Spain's Ishbilia and Granada, Cairo, Tunis, Jerusalem and many others.[20] In fact, the oldest university in the world is Al-Azhar in Cairo, Egypt. The point is that all these students and scholars were proud and happy to be educated and articulate in the Arabic language because it is the language which **ALLAH** (*subhanahu wa ta'ala*) used to spread His Word.

If you want to learn Islam then you have to learn Arabic. The authors have spent a great deal of effort to use the authentic Arabic terms in this and other books to express meanings of **ALLAH**'s (*subhanahu wa ta'ala*) Word in their original, authentic form. Though we put the English translation along with the Arabic, it has to be explicitly and implicitly asserted that the English counterpart of the Arabic is not an example *par excellence* of the Arabic. The **Generous Qur'an,** is the actual, authentic Word of **ALLAH** (*subhanahu wa ta'ala*) and is beyond the limited human conception, even though some humans can understand, in part, some of the meaning. (**ALLAH** (*subhanahu wa ta'ala*) knows best.) This is why the **Qur'anic** Arabic is crucial to read and understand, and this English text is only an auxiliary addition for those who are devoid of understanding of the Arabic language, the language which **ALLAH** (*subhanahu wa ta'ala*) chose to deliver His message to humankind. In our opinion, people should only read the book of **ALLAH** (*subhanahu wa ta'ala*), the **Generous Qur'an** and the *hadith*, because everything is contained within them. The Light, pearls and jewels speak for themselves. What we, the authors, have written is no more than an attempt to write a book that explains the contradictions of the times in an endeavor to call to the guidance of Islam whomever **ALLAH** (*subhanahu wa ta'ala*) permits to hear and read it, in the hope that **ALLAH** (*subhanahu wa ta'ala*) will forgive us and provide for us in this life and the next. This is what Muslims were encouraged to do by our **Prophet Muhammad** (*prayers and peace of **ALLAH** be upon him*).

57

Endnotes

[1]Theodora Bynon, *Historical Linguistics*, (Cambridge, England: Cambridge University Press, 1986), pp. 34-89.

[2]E.C. Gracia, "Quantity into Quality: Synchronic Indeterminacy and Language Change", *Lingua*, 65, pp. 275-306.

[3]Bynon, Op. Cit., pp. 7-9.

[4]Anwar G. Chejne, *The Arabic Language: Its Role in History*, (Minneapolis, MN: University of Minnesota Press: 1969), pp. 3-24.

[5]David S. Miall, "The Indeterminacy of Literary Texts: The View from the Reader", *Journal of Literary Semantics*, XVII/3 (November, 1988), pp. 155-171.

[6]Ibid.

[7]Brigitte Nerlich and David C. Clarke, "A Dynamic Model of Semantic Change", *Journal of Literary Semantics*, XVII/2 (August, 1988), pp. 73-90.

[8]Gracia, Op. Cit.

[9]Bynon, Op. Cit., p. 266.

وَوَهَبْنَا لَهُم مِّن رَّحْمَتِنَا وَجَعَلْنَا لَهُمْ لِسَانَ صِدْقٍ عَلِيّاً ۝

58

[10]Miall, Op. Cit.

[11]Chejne, Op. Cit.

[12]Ibid.

[13]Bynon, Op. Cit., pp. 196-256.

[14]Philip K. Hitti, *History of the Arabs: From the Earliest Times to the Present*, (London: Macmillan and Co., 1970), pp. 617-694.

[15]Bynon, Op. Cit..

[16]Ibid.

[17]Hitti, Op. Cit., pp. 3-79.

[18]Reynold A. Nicholson, *A Literary History of the Arabs,* (Cambridge, England: Cambridge University Press, 1962), pp. 71-140.

[19]Ibid.

[20]Hitti, Op. Cit., pp. 408-415.

Tawki

59

CHAPTER III

The Generous Qur'an *Pari Passu* The Word of ALLAH (*subhanahu wa ta'ala*)

Introduction

It is imperative to understand that the **Generous Qur'an** can only really be understood, in its autonomous contextual dimensions, in Arabic. When **ALLAH** (*subhanahu wa ta'ala*) guides a person, He gives him or her Light in order to understand His Word. Through that understanding, the Light will reveal itself. The jewels will become crystal and the pearls will start to glow. A verse of the **Generous Qur'an** explains itself by itself. Simultaneously, a verse or a word may be explained by another verse or word, and the meaning of one verse or word may be hidden by another through its allegorical, chronological and punctuation dimensions. All of this shines an infinite Light. There is an urgent need to understand what the Arabic word means. **ALLAH** (*subhanahu wa ta'ala*) has already taught Adam the names of all things. The exposé now turns to a focus on the phenomena of names from the Islamic perspective.

What's in a name? Shakespeare typified one answer to his question in his line "a rose by any other name would smell as sweet". In this view, the rose is a reality that is only arbitrarily

60

symbolized in the subjective mind by the letters r-o-s-e. The word is seen as merely a bridge or a representative image linking reality with human consciousness. Otherwise, the two are infinitely separated. The word itself has no independent meaning. This concept is at the basis of a whole civilization.[1]

Each society's perspective of words and naming is of vital importance to its whole relationship to reality: its belief and its *praxis*, its norms and its patterns, its ends and its means. The human relationship to words is a microcosm for human life in general, because it occupies a central, initiating and defining position in all other realms, and because it embodies human motivations, aspirations, intentions and attitudes. Every society places the names of what is most important to it in the forefront of its consciousness. Thus, even in a society that supposes itself to be concerned with only materialistically verifiable facts and "hard realities", the unquantifiable realm of names and other words is the medium in which people act. In the words of Walt Whitman, "Words and deeds are quite indifferent modes of the divine energy. Words are also actions, and actions are a kind of words."[2]

Whether they are true or not, words are the world in which people dwell. Words cannot be separated from any other reality. As Paul Ricoeur pointed out, there is no basis for seeing the world as separate from the word, the physical thing called a rose from the sound of its name. "If language does not exist for itself, but in view of the world that it opens up and uncovers, then the interpretation of language is not distinct from the interpretation of the world".[3] The unity of the word and the world is very important for understanding the Islamic perspective of words and naming. This essay seeks to describe this perspective based primarily on the

61

Islamic belief in the **Generous Qur'an** as God's Word. To this end, it will first be important to clarify Islam's view of the Divine Word *vis-à-vis* all other types of words, after which the role of the word in Muslim practice and piety will be briefly discussed. Finally, **Qur'anic** and other Islamic sources will be analyzed for an explanation of the fundamental principles of the Islamic view of the Divine Word and its role in human life.

Man's Understanding of Divine Transcendence

In any discussion of naming and religion in general and Islam in particular, it is imperative to understand that the divine origin and referent of the Name is transcendent. The concept of divine transcendence is often believed to have its foundation in the idea of that which is holy, which Rudolf Otto called the "innermost core" of all religious belief. Despite the great variation in interpretations of the meaning of the word "holy" it seems to have as one major theme the otherness or separation of the holy from the non-holy. The philosopher W. Donald Hudson suggests that there are two major views on divine transcendence as a theological concept, each of which has a particular relationship to religious words and naming.

One view states that the transcendence or separation of that which is holy can be put into words. The other view states that it cannot. The crux of the matter from Hudson's point of view is that holiness, according to Otto's framework is in itself a "verbally indefinable otherness". This is the basis for Otto's category of the "numenous", or that which is completely outside of man's capability to understand by way of concepts and their descriptions.

62

Chapter III. The Generous Qur'an *Pari Passu* the Word of ALLAH

Hudson goes on to distinguish between two possible implications of this notion of the transcendence of the holy. First, it is possible that as an empirical fact, man by nature is simply incapable of the knowledge necessary to describe the holy. The second possible implication is that by a logical inference, human linguistic processes provide no means for a coherent description of the holy.

The central question that both of these interpretations imply is "Can God be coherently described in human language as ordinarily used?"[4] One of the conceptions described above states that the answer is yes, meaning that language is capable of being used for a description of God, but man's knowledge can never arrive at the stage where it would be capable of producing such a description without severe limitations. Thus, in this view, God is "beyond knowledge". The other view posited by Hudson is that God is "beyond description" due to the shortcomings of human language. In the first case, God is not beyond all description, for man may describe to the limited extent that he understands. That is, man's speech about God is limited by man's lack of knowledge. In the second case, God is indeed considered beyond all description because human language as ordinarily used is incapable of transmitting coherent meaning about the realm of the holy. In this case, man's speech about God is prevented by its sheer impossibility.

Hudson describes several different grounds for the "beyond description" argument about divine transcendence. The first one he calls the empirical ground. This argument states that religious experience is by nature ineffable and therefore beyond words. There is no way that people trying to describe their ineffable experiences to each other could have certainty that they are talking about the same thing. Rudolf Otto can be seen as representing this type of claim.

The second type of ground for claiming that God is "beyond description" is, according to Hudson, the semantic ground. This claim is based on certain theories of meaning which state that verbal expression regarding the divine is void of significance. Therefore, if there is something that is divine, it must exist, again, beyond the realm of words.

Finally, Hudson states that there is a theological ground for claiming that divine transcendence is beyond description. In simple terms, this theological argument claims that because God is infinite and man's conception is finite, then everything man says about God must be outside the bounds of logic and sense. The "Church Father" Tertullian's maxim *credo quia absurdum* (meaning, "I believe because it is absurd"), applied to his support of the historical Christian doctrine of the "trinity", is a classical example of this notion. What this means is that self-contradiction is to be expected in the truth about God.[5] Since God is not bound by human norms of logic or expectations, then humans must "simply believe" when they are confronted with doctrines that seem to go against the grain of their common sense.

The net result of these claims about divine transcendence has been a type of representational conception of the words used to describe God, whereby these words describe the analogues of certain qualities, rather than God Himself. In addition, there is a popular view in modern times that religious expression, while it may be incoherent from the point of view of objective meaning, does play a role in the subjective experience of the individual participant.

Hudson presents a "beyond knowledge" approach to divine transcendence as an alternative to these types of "beyond description" approaches. He suggests that when people claim that

64

no description of God can be true, they are negating the basic assumption that God is transcendent.[6]

The Lexicon for Describing God

It is a much considered point in the Western philosophy of religion that human language is a medium incapable of expressing in a coherent and lasting way the experience of divine transcendence.[7] What this means is that the human word is too feeble a thing to describe or name God. From the Islamic perspective, the only proper words to describe God are those that He reveals about Himself and are preserved in the **Generous Qur'an**. Therefore, any language other than Arabic and any lexicon other than Islamic lexicon in **Qur'anic** Arabic will not be sufficient tools for describing God. This is because humanity does not have the knowledge to describe God separate from humanity's own manipulation of words. As well, it is because historical human language is not a sufficient tool for use in describing reality and experience in a way that will do justice to its transcendent objective reality. Human intellectual deliberation has to articulate its perspective of reality in a form of human language. This is due to the fact that the human intellect is to a certain extent encapsulated within the illusionary interplay between space and time. The syntax and semantics of human speech are limited by human capabilities. Human consciousness can never encompass God's consciousness and thereby humans are incapable of objectively describing the unfathomable.

From the Islamic perspective, the only way that the unfathomable and the beyond, *pari passu* the infinite power of God

65

could be described and thereby understood is by His infinite Word in the same way He referred to Himself.[8]

The Islamic Perspective of Words

An introduction to the Islamic perspective of words will convey this immediacy of the rule of the Divine Word as crucial to everything about Islam. Islam's emphasis on *tawhid*, or Oneness, is manifested in the unity between the Divine Word and the multiplicity of reality.

A spoken tradition of our **Prophet Muhammad** (*prayers and peace of* **ALLAH** *be upon him*) tells us to "Read the **Qur'an**, because it will come on the Day of Judgment as a mediator (or intercessor) for its companions". This statement is extremely important for understanding how the Divine Word functions as a medium of reality. The Divine Word is not first and foremost to be understood intellectually. This will provide no access to its secrets and its benefits. Rather it is to be practiced as a way of life. In his discourses, Jalaluddin Rumi presents as a metaphor for the **Generous Qur'an** the example of a beautiful bride who veils herself. If one is too eager to tear away the veil, penetrate to the secrets of the bride and enjoy them without having to sacrifice and work for them, thus proving one's love, devotion and persistence, then the bride will show herself as ugly so that one will not find a desire to continue his quest. On the other hand, if a person is willing to serve the bride from afar, while he patiently and humbly, tends her flocks and fields in daily chores, etc., (i.e., practicing a patient

66

"remembrance", with no presumption of penetrating any secrets) then the bride will invite him herself and reveal herself to him.[9]

This metaphor reflects the unique role of the word and the name in Islamic piety. The word is not something to be added to the memory banks as a unit of acquired knowledge, or something that could be bought with tuition fees, etc. It is something that must be practiced from day to day so that a person will be transformed in the process. It is revealed in part to the human being in the course of experiences, not acquired from outside in a process of memorization or analysis. In this context, life itself becomes inseparable from the word, because each event, whether it brings joy or suffering, must be encountered with a divine word, in the reciting of which the individual accepts that all things occur as a result of God's Will and Plan. This acceptance is a key aspect of submission in itself, which is Islam.[10]

(It should be noted that the authors' capitalization of the term "word" is for the most part reserved for those cases in which the Divine Word, as it is understood in the Islamic and not the Christian sense, is referred to in a general and not a specific manner.)

The Changing Dimensions of Human Words

This description and understanding is not applied only to the beyond but also to every aspect of the physical, contemporaneous reality. In both cases, it is understood from the Islamic perspective that no one intellect and/or group of intellects could ever articulate what man's understanding and action should be from an objective point of view, because they are the prisoners of their historical inculcation. In addition, they may be limited by their own analytical capability, which is most of the time a victim of the phenomenon of compartmentalization. Every human paradigm, every human perspective and every human word lacks the objective *furqan* (criterion for the sharp edge of discrepancy) and thereby cannot explain reality with an enduring authority. Therefore, because human wording cannot explain reality *in toto*, one finds in retrospect that human wording and naming *per se* as tools of analysis, description and understanding, have constituted no more than the changing variables of history.

On the other hand, from the Islamic perspective, the only surviving Word in history is the **Generous Qur'an**. This is not only because of the efforts of the Arabs and Muslims. It is unequivocally and irrevocably because **ALLAH** (*subhanahu wa ta'ala*) made the commitment upon Himself to preserve the **Generous Qur'an** in Arabic. **ALLAH** (*subhanahu wa ta'ala*) did not preserve only the **Generous Qur'an**, but also preserved the Arabic language, which became a medium for understanding the infallible Word of God. Therefore, according to the Islamic consciousness, to understand the beyond as well as contemporaneous and historical conditions, it is only necessary to consult the authentic wording and naming of **ALLAH** (*subhanahu wa ta'ala*) found in the **Generous Qur'an**. The **Generous Qur'an** is likened to a boat in which a person can travel back and forth through time, because when **ALLAH** (*subhanahu wa ta'ala*) reveals one sentence, it governs the human trajectory. It is thus seen as applicable to every human community, regardless of its time dimension. Only the Word of God can define, for the Muslims, all human beings and all things, what is going on in every society, as well as the order of things. The secret is in the

68

Word, and the Word is a medium for meaning. The meaning is
embedded in the Divine Name. Finally, the Name has infinite
depth that opens unto a pious true believer infinite realms of reality
which the rational deliberation of others can never imagine.[11]

The Word of Allah as the Abiding Force of History

Within these notions, no common ground exists between
names as **ALLAH** (*subhanahu wa ta'ala*) referred to them as versus
names that were constructed and concocted by humans. Though
only Muslims recognize the infinite dimension of the **Generous
Qur'an**, Muslims as well as non-Muslims look to any *ayah* (verse)
in the **Generous Qur'an**, to any word of the **Generous Qur'an**, to
any meaning of the word, and they recognize their impotence to
ever hope to contrive such words on their own. When a person
starts, with an initial level of Islamic consciousness, to read and
understand the **Generous Qur'an**, he eventually finds out that he is
not really reading the **Generous Qur'an** but the **Generous Qur'an** is
reading him, invading and navigating through his chest and heart,
letting him start on the infinite journey of ideational
metamorphosis as a prelude to understanding the depth of one
letter, one name, one word, one verse, one breath, one period. This
is why **ALLAH** (*subhanahu wa ta'ala*) referred to the **Generous
Qur'an**, first as being generous in its meaning and second as full of
hidden secrets. Each name and word has an outward apparent
meaning and simultaneously has a hidden meaning. It is the pious
human Islamic consciousness that becomes the inward and
outward linkage of some of these infinite meanings.[12]

Chapter III. The Generous Qur'an *Pari Passu* the Word of ALLAH

Each word in the **Generous Qur'an** becomes a refuge to all human beings because it constitutes what is called *furqan* ("criterion"). This *furqan* establishes in itself the demarcation line between what constitutes good and what constitutes bad.[13] The Word of **ALLAH** (*subhanahu wa ta'ala*) in itself is an infinite treasure, and piety is required to unveil some of these treasures. Finally it is imperative to understand that in the beginning, what *is* is nothingness and the exception to this nothingness is **ALLAH** (*subhanahu wa ta'ala*). Through **ALLAH's** (*subhanahu wa ta'ala*) Word, creation became. The creation is the outcome of the order of **ALLAH** (*subhanahu wa ta'ala*) through the Word. The Word became the existent reality. The Word, through the name, became no more than a linkage between negation and reality. Every aspect of creation has a name and every name has an image. Every image through its name became an existent reality. To understand reality, we have to understand the name. From the Islamic perspective, those successful people with piety can inwardly and outwardly see the congruity between the name and reality.[14]

Because **ALLAH** (*subhanahu wa ta'ala*) taught Adam "all the names", imbedded inside every human being is *a priori* knowledge of all names. Therefore, when a person comes to the consciousness of knowing or learning something, he is not learning something new. He is only remembering his original human estate which holds *a priori* knowledge. Everything in physical reality is no more than a medium, an example to remind people of the knowledge that they already have. Through observation, a person is not seeing something new, but he is seeing the name that **ALLAH** (*subhanahu wa ta'ala*) has already imbedded in him. One has to remember that

70

from the Islamic perspective all existence is already within all men
and that in them the Word indeed became flesh.[15]

The Role of the Generous Qur'an in Islamic Practice

Islam is the only authentic reality. Thereby from an Islamic
point of view, no man, whether Muslim or non-Muslim, is capable
of describing **ALLAH** (*subhanahu wa ta'ala*) with words, concepts or
names introduced independently from the Word of **ALLAH**
(*subhanahu wa ta'ala*) as manifested in the **Generous Qur'an**. Man
is indeed incapable of fully knowing God. In addition, man's use of
language is an insufficient tool for describing God's transcendence.
This is only an indication of the power and immediacy of God's
Word, *pari passu* the **Generous Qur'an**, within Islamic society.

While it is not necessary for the purposes of this essay to
launch into an extended account of the permeation of the Divine
Word at all levels of Islamic life, some examples are helpful. The
center of all aspects of Islamic *praxis* is the Word. Islamic ritual
centers on recitation of the **Generous Qur'an**. The written and
spoken Word of **ALLAH** (*subhanahu wa ta'ala*) is attended to with
concentration, letter by letter. Attention to each letter has a
meaning which is at the crux of the matter for understanding the
role of the Divine Word in Islam. A tradition of our **Prophet
Muhammad** (*prayers and peace of* **ALLAH** *be upon him*) states that
"Whosoever reads one letter from the Book of ALLAH will have
reward, and the reward is equal to ten times; I am not saying that
Alif Lam Mim is one letter, but Alif is one letter, Lam is one letter
and Mim is one letter".

71

Chapter III. The Generous Qur'an *Pari Passu* the Word of ALLAH

All daily activities are prefaced and concluded with remembrances of the Name of God, such as in the continuous recitation of *"Bismi ALLAHI Al-Rahmani Al-Rahim"* (meaning, "By the Name of **ALLAH**, the Most Compassionate, the Most Merciful"), the saying of *"insha'***ALLAH***"* ("with the Will of **ALLAH**"--*subhanahu wa ta'ala*) in reference to plans for the future, greetings between Muslims, saying *"Al-Hamdu Lillah"* ("Thanks be to **ALLAH**"--*subhanahu wa ta'ala*)after eating and drinking, etc. Islamic architecture is traditionally decorated with calligraphic quotations from the **Generous Qur'an**, and is fundamentally concerned with the acoustic needs of those who are listening to **Generous Qur'anic** recitation.[16] **Qur'anic** recitation is a primary form of Islamic "entertainment" and is refined to a very exacting art in many Islamic lands, including non-Arab countries such as Indonesia. Finally, traditional Islamic scholarship of all kinds is usually based upon the **Generous Qur'an** and verses thereof which are relevant to the topic of study. In fact, Islamic scholarship in its totality can be considered a search for greater proximity to **ALLAH** (*subhanahu wa ta'ala*) through His Word. Therefore, study of any phenomenon can be considered a study of the **Generous Qur'an**, because all of creation is the result of the Word. In exploring one, the scholar is exploring the other. The **Generous Qur'an** makes continual reference to *"ayat"*, or signs, not only in the Book itself but in all of creation, since as mentioned above, every created thing is a result of God's command to "Be!" For example, in *Surah Al-'Imran, ayah* 190, **ALLAH** (*subhanahu wa ta'ala*) says, "Surely in the creation of the heavens and the earth, and in the alternation of night and day are signs for men of understanding". Every aspect of creation is thus a sign of God, though most humans may not see

72

this and are living in a realm of fragmented vision by which they may see things as substantially distinct from one another in the realm of meaning. Another verse in the **Generous Qur'an** points out that "There is nothing that does not proclaim His glory, but you do not understand their glorification".

* *

SURAH III (3) *The Family
of 'Imran*

190. Lo! In the creation of the heavens and the earth and (in) the difference of night and day are tokens (of His sovereignty) for men of understanding.

إِنَّ فِى خَلْقِ السَّمَوَٰتِ وَالْأَرْضِ وَاخْتِلَٰفِ الَّيْلِ وَالنَّهَارِ لَآيَٰتٍ لِأُولِى الْأَلْبَابِ ۝

III *Surah Ali-'Imran*, **The Generous Qur'an** 3:190

* *

SURAH XVII (17) *The Night Journey*

44. The seven heavens and the earth and all that is therein praise Him, and there is not a thing but hymneth His praise; but ye understand not their praise. Lo! He is ever Clement, Forgiving.

تُسَبِّحُ لَهُ السَّمَوَٰتُ السَّبْعُ وَالْأَرْضُ وَمَن فِيهِنَّ وَإِن مِّن شَىْءٍ إِلَّا يُسَبِّحُ بِحَمْدِهِ وَلَٰكِن لَّا تَفْقَهُونَ تَسْبِيحَهُمْ إِنَّهُ كَانَ حَلِيمًا غَفُورًا ۝

XVII *Surah Al-Israa'*, **The Generous Qur'an** 17:44

* *

73

Accordingly, human beings can potentially see in themselves the totality of reality. A *hadith* of our **Prophet Muhammad** (*prayers and peace of* **ALLAH** *be upon him*) says: "Whoso knows his own self knows his Lord".[17] Ultimately the Word begins and ends in the same place. As it has been the secret of the creation of man in the first place upon the Form of **ALLAH** (*subhanahu wa ta'ala*), so in the end, through the Islamic *praxis* of the Word through *thikr* (remembrance), it reintegrates him into his original essence (*fitrah*).

The Generous Qur'an, *Pari Passu* the Word of Allah

It is imperative to understand that from the Islamic perspective, the Word is the medium of reality. The Word in itself, through its verbatim and conceptual meaning, is congruent with the order of things. According to Islam, the world of existence is no more than a divine word, and that word consists of letters which become a creative world.[18] That is to say, the diametrical world of existence corresponds to letters of the language. "Verily, when He intends a thing, His command is "Be" and it is!"

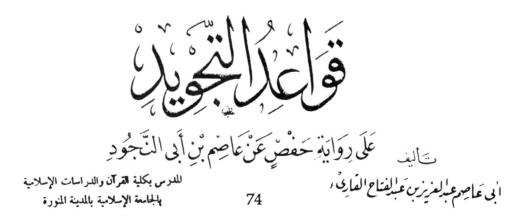

74

****

SURAH XXXVI (36) *Ya Sin*

82. But His command, when He intendeth a thing, is only that he saith unto it: Be! and it is.

إِنَّمَآ أَمْرُهُ إِذَآ أَرَادَ شَيْئًا أَن يَقُولَ لَهُ كُن فَيَكُونُ ۝

XXXVI *Surah Ya Sin*, **The Generous Qur'an** 36:82

****

Simply put, when **ALLAH** (*subhanahu wa ta'ala*) wants to create something, He only says *"kun"*, and that thing comes into existence. This word, which in Arabic consists of two letters, is a divine order from **ALLAH** (*subhanahu wa ta'ala*). The result of this divine order, made through the word, is the existence of a world: a world of being, a world of perfection, a world of completed existence. The things that human beings can conceive of through their faculties, the things that they cannot conceive of, all things that are in the universe, the realms of existence at all levels of stratification, are no more than the net result of the divine order of **ALLAH** (*subhanahu wa ta'ala*) through the word *"kun"*. This means that prior to existence, what is and what was, is the word, and **ALLAH's** (*subhanahu wa ta'ala*) Word is an order. When **ALLAH** (*subhanahu wa ta'ala*) gives an order through a word, the word becomes a world of existence.

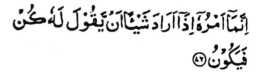

حُجَّةُ الْإِسْلَامِ مُحَمَّدِ بْنِ أَبِي حَامِدِ الْغَزَالِي

75

The Arabic, Qur'anic and Islamic Paradigm:
Light, Jewels and Pearls

Chapter III. The Generous Qur'an *Pari Passu* the Word of ALLAH

★★

<u>SURAH XXXVI (36)</u> *Ya Sin*

83. Therefore glory be to Him in Whose hand is the dominion over all things! Unto Him ye will be brought back.

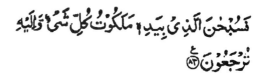

XXXVI *Surah Ya Sin,* **The Generous Qur'an** 36:83

★★

The realm of existence is no more than the net result of the words of **ALLAH** (*subhanahu wa ta'ala*). These words are infinite and sovereign. It is impossible for human faculties to grasp their sovereignty, because they originated from **ALLAH** (*subhanahu wa ta'ala*), and human consciousness can never encompass God's consciousness. In actuality, it is **ALLAH** (*subhanahu wa ta'ala*) Who invades and navigates through the human consciousness and faculties, and directs and orders them to whatever **ALLAH** (*subhanahu wa ta'ala*) wants. The words of **ALLAH** (*subhanahu wa ta'ala*) are infinite, and to bring this infinity to human consciousness, **ALLAH** (*subhanahu wa ta'ala*) gives the allegorical analogy that if one brought all the trees of the Earth and used them as pens, and used the ocean as ink, with seven seas behind it to add to it, the latter would be exhausted and finished before the Word of **ALLAH** (*subhanahu wa ta'ala*) was finished.

76

****

<u>SURAH XXXI (31)</u> *Luqman*

27. And if all the trees in the earth were pens, and the sea, with seven more seas to help it, (were ink), the words of Allah could not be exhausted. Lo! Allah is Mighty, Wise.

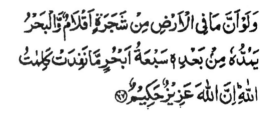

XXXI *Luqman*, **The Generous Qur'an** 31:27

****

The Word of **ALLAH** (*subhanahu wa ta'ala*) in itself is the medium of existence. This Word was originated by **ALLAH** (*subhanahu wa ta'ala*) and is exemplified in the Arabic language by the word *"kun"*. The net result of the Arabic word *"kun"* is creation: a homeostatic and infinite system. This system, with its multiplicity of meanings, has imbedded in it many realms. One of these realms is the realm of spirit, another is the realm of image. Thus, the net result of the divinely ordained word of *"kun"* is all the worlds, with their infinite realms of appearance. So matter itself is a result of the word of **ALLAH** (*subhanahu wa ta'ala*). Everything that *is* is a result of a word from **ALLAH** (*subhanahu wa ta'ala*). Accordingly, from the Islamic perspective, no person can ever try to understand the order of things and the order of the world without understanding the divinely ordained Word of **ALLAH** (*subhanahu wa ta'ala*) in Arabic. Thus, Muslim scholars

77

have stated in many instances that the only authentic source and medium of reality is the **Generous Qur'an** in Arabic. Historically, as has been mentioned, many non-Arab scholars of the world learned the Arabic language in the anticipation of understanding the **Generous Qur'an** in Arabic.[19]

Thus, in Islamic scholarship there is no higher value than studying and hearing the authentic Word of **ALLAH** (*subhanahu wa ta'ala*). This type of scholarship is not the province of only a few in the society, because even the uneducated and unlettered are equipped to understand it at one level or another. This is because **ALLAH** (*subhanahu wa ta'ala*) created humanity with certain faculties so that it could understand **ALLAH's** (*subhanahu wa ta'ala*) Word with ease. In the first few verses of *Surah Al-Baqqara*, the **Generous Qur'an** is described as being a guide to those with *taqwa* (piety), who truly believe in and practice Islam.

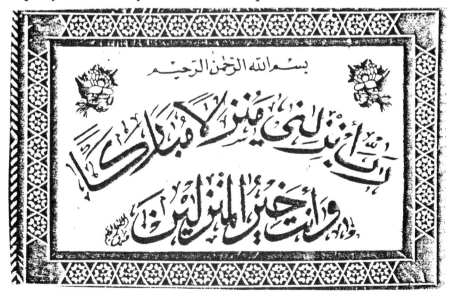

78

****

SURAH II (2) *The Cow*

In the name of Allah, the Beneficent,
the Merciful.

1. Alif. Lam. Mim.

2. This is the Scripture wherein there
is no doubt, a guidance unto those
who ward off (evil):

3. Who believe in the unseen, and
establish worship, and spend of that
We have bestowed upon them;

4. And who believe in that which is
revealed unto thee (Muhammad) and
that which was revealed before thee,
and are certain of the Hereafter.

5. These depend on guidance from
their Lord. These are the successful.

ايٰتها (٢) سُوۡرَةُ الۡبَقَرَةِ مَدَنِيَّةٌ رُكُوۡعَاتُهَا

بِسۡمِ اللّٰهِ الرَّحۡمٰنِ الرَّحِیۡمِ ۝

الٓمّٓ ۝

ذٰلِكَ الۡكِتٰبُ لَا رَيۡبَ فِيۡهِ هُدًى لِّلۡمُتَّقِيۡنَ ۝

الَّذِيۡنَ يُؤۡمِنُوۡنَ بِالۡغَيۡبِ وَ يُقِيۡمُوۡنَ الصَّلٰوةَ وَمِمَّا رَزَقۡنٰهُمۡ يُنۡفِقُوۡنَ ۝

وَالَّذِيۡنَ يُؤۡمِنُوۡنَ بِمَا اُنۡزِلَ اِلَيۡكَ وَمَا اُنۡزِلَ مِنۡ قَبۡلِكَ وَبِالۡاٰخِرَةِ هُمۡ يُوۡقِنُوۡنَ ۝

اُولٰٓئِكَ عَلٰى هُدًى مِّنۡ رَّبِّهِمۡ وَاُولٰٓئِكَ هُمُ الۡمُفۡلِحُوۡنَ ۝

II *Surah Al-Baqqara,* **The Generous Qur'an** 2:1-5

****

Thus, to be able to understand the Word of **ALLAH** (*subhanahu wa ta'ala*), man, who is a result of that Word, has first and foremost to become conscious that he is *'abd*, a slave. A slave, not to the human mind, but to **ALLAH** (*subhanahu wa ta'ala*). At that point, when man becomes conscious that he is *'abd* **ALLAH** (*subhanahu wa ta'ala*), he is in the realm of reality in which he could appreciate the infinite depth of **ALLAH's** (*subhanahu wa ta'ala*) Word. He finds that the worlds of existence, including the realm of being and the realm of images, etc., are no more than words that have originated with **ALLAH** (*subhanahu wa ta'ala*).[20]

Man's *A Priori* Knowledge Through the Divine Word

ALLAH's (*subhanahu wa ta'ala*) word *"kun"* created humankind. Adam was in the realm of "things", a conglomeration of sand, clay and water, etc. When the order of **ALLAH** (*subhanahu wa ta'ala*), *"kun"*, came to this conglomeration of things, Adam became a human. Adam was thus created through the divine word *"kun"*, through which he entered the realm of being. The word *"kun"* is the same divinely ordained word which created the world. Therefore, this complete human being has embedded within him the aggregation of the universe itself. Thus it is said that man became the microcosm of the creation. Embedded in man are the aggregate realities of the world as well as the Word, because the two are identical. Significantly, it is said in the **Generous Qur'an** to this effect that **ALLAH** (*subhanahu wa ta'ala*) taught Adam the aggregation of all the names.

80

Chapter III. The Generous Qur'an *Pari Passu* the Word of ALLAH

****

SURAH II (2) *The Cow*

31. And He taught Adam all the names, then showed them to the angels, saying: Inform me of the names of these if ye are truthful.

32. They said: Be glorified! We have no knowledge saving that which Thou hast taught us. Lo! Thou, only Thou, art the Knower, the Wise.

33. He said: O Adam! Inform them of their names, and when he had informed them of their names, He said: Did I not tell you that I know the secret of the heavens and the earth? And I know that which ye disclose and which ye hide.

وَعَلَّمَ ءَادَمَ الْأَسْمَاءَ كُلَّهَا ثُمَّ عَرَضَهُمْ عَلَى الْمَلَٰٓئِكَةِ
فَقَالَ أَنۢبِـُٔونِى بِأَسْمَاءِ هَٰٓؤُلَاءِ إِن كُنتُمْ
صَٰدِقِينَ ۩
قَالُوا۟ سُبْحَٰنَكَ لَا عِلْمَ لَنَآ إِلَّا مَا عَلَّمْتَنَآ إِنَّكَ أَنتَ
الْعَلِيمُ الْحَكِيمُ ۩
قَالَ يَٰٓـَٔادَمُ أَنۢبِئْهُم بِأَسْمَآئِهِمْ فَلَمَّآ أَنۢبَأَهُم بِأَسْمَآئِهِمْ
قَالَ أَلَمْ أَقُل لَّكُمْ إِنِّىٓ أَعْلَمُ غَيْبَ السَّمَٰوَٰتِ وَالْأَرْضِ
وَأَعْلَمُ مَا تُبْدُونَ وَمَا كُنتُمْ تَكْتُمُونَ ۩

II *Surah Al-Baqqara*, **The Generous Qur'an** 2:31-33

****

Chapter III. The Generous Qur'an *Pari Passu* the Word of ALLAH

Imbedded in Adam is the aggregation of the words of **ALLAH** (*subhanahu wa ta'ala*) because **ALLAH** (*subhanahu wa ta'ala*) taught him the names of all things, without limitation. The names themselves become parallel and equivalent to the realms of existence with their multiplicity of beings. That is to say, humankind becomes a small microscopic system that corresponds to the infinite macroscopic system of the worlds. Man himself becomes an indicator of that infinite world. He becomes a symbolic manifestation of the realities of the worlds. Therefore, man becomes a linkage between two separate, yet interrelated and integrated realms. He becomes a demarcation line between what *is* and what is being created. What *is* refers to **ALLAH** (*subhanahu wa ta'ala*). What is being created through the Word is the universe in its totality. Thus, man in himself is the demarcation line, and has no existence without **ALLAH** (*subhanahu wa ta'ala*).[21]

It is imperative to understand that while man, *pari passu,* 'abd **ALLAH** (*subhanahu wa ta'ala*), is separate from **ALLAH** (*subhanahu wa ta'ala*), man has embedded in him the aggregation of the Word of **ALLAH** (*subhanahu wa ta'ala*). Man becomes a medium of this aggregation. Therefore, he is not really separate from God, but his existence, the human estate, becomes a linkage between **ALLAH** (*subhanahu wa ta'ala*) and His creation. Man's existence gives a *de facto* proof, a symbolic indicator, that nothing can come into being without a word from **ALLAH** (*subhanahu wa ta'ala*), because by that word, God created man. The Word has become a real existence, a unity between spirit and matter, a unity between the inward and outward manifestations of reality. Therefore, man's existence has a dual symbolic meaning, one as separate from God and one as in unity with the Word of God,

82

which is embedded in man. **ALLAH** (*subhanahu wa ta'ala*) mentions in the **Generous Qur'an** that His signs will be demonstrated in all aspects of creation, including what is very distant as well as what is within man himself. The **Generous Qur'an** itself is made up of verses that are called *ayat*, and in addition, the *ayat* exist throughout the created world. Thus, again, the world and the Word are one.

* *

SURAH XLI (41) *Fusilat*

53. We shall show then Our portents on the horizons and within themselves until it will be manifest unto them that it is the Truth. Doth not thy Lord suffice, since He is Witness over all things?

سَنُرِيهِمْ ايَـٰتِنَا فِى الْاٰفَاقِ وَفِىٓ اَنْفُسِهِمْ حَتّٰى يَتَبَيَّنَ لَهُمْ اَنَّهُ الْحَقُّ اَوَلَمْ يَكْفِ بِرَبِّكَ اَنَّهُ عَلٰى كُلِّ شَىْءٍ شَهِيدٌ ۝

XLI *Surah Ha Mim Al-Sajdah*, **The Generous Qur'an** 41:53

* *

According to the first four *ayat* of *Surah Al-Rahman*, it was after **ALLAH** (*subhanahu wa ta'ala*) had taught the **Generous Qur'an** that He created man. Then, after **ALLAH** (*subhanahu wa ta'ala*) created man, He taught him the clarity of vision in which to understand **ALLAH's** (*subhanahu wa ta'ala*) Words. As described above, **ALLAH's** (*subhanahu wa ta'ala*) Word is inside and equivalent to man. **ALLAH** (*subhanahu wa ta'ala*) taught man

83

Chapter III. The Generous Qur'an *Pari Passu* the Word of ALLAH

vision and proper deliberation, and gave him the consciousness to understand the Word of **ALLAH** (*subhanahu wa ta'ala*). The Word of **ALLAH** (*subhanahu wa ta'ala*) thus unites man with his vision. When a human being comes to grips with the fact that he is *'abd* **ALLAH** (*subhanahu wa ta'ala*), his vision starts to understand the infinite words and worlds embedded within himself. Thus the **Generous Qur'an** becomes a linkage between **ALLAH** (*subhanahu wa ta'ala*) and man. Simultaneously, the **Generous Qur'an** becomes the criterion for the delineation between man and God. This is according to the chronological order of the verses of *Surah Al-Rahman, ayat* 1-4:

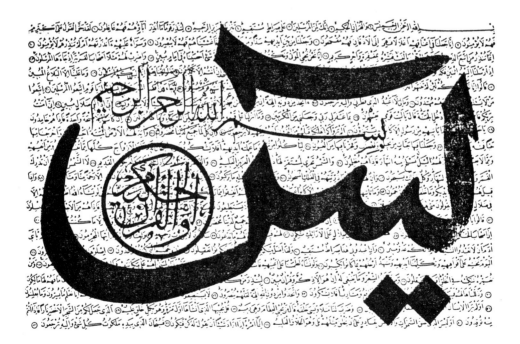

84

****

<u>SURAH LV (55)</u> *The Beneficent*

In the name of Allah, the Beneficent,
the Merciful.

بِسْمِ اللهِ الرَّحْمٰنِ الرَّحِيْمِ ۝

الرَّحْمٰنُ ۝
1. The Beneficent

عَلَّمَ الْقُرْاٰنَ ۝
2. Hath made known the Qur'an.

خَلَقَ الْاِنْسَانَ ۝
3. He hath created men,

عَلَّمَهُ الْبَيَانَ ۝
4. He hath taught him utterance.

LV *Surah Al-Rahman*, **The Generous Qur'an** 55:1-4

****

The Similarity Between Man and The Generous Qur'an

The **Generous Qur'an** in Arabic, from this perspective, has an existence similar and parallel to humankind. The **Generous Qur'an** as the Word of God is the aggregate of the multiplicity of creation and being, and thus is similar to man, in whom is also embedded the Word of God. The Word of God is not governed by the illusionary interplay between space and time, and thus is timeless

85

Chapter III. The Generous Qur'an *Pari Passu* the Word of ALLAH

while simultaneously being compatible with the contemporaneous existence of every time and place. Thus conscious individuals and true believers can see it in every dimension of their immediate application. In fact, the Word of **ALLAH** (*subhanahu wa ta'ala*) is seen as the only relevant and proper word for humans to say. As the great Islamic scholar Ibn Taymiyah stated, "The origin of the misguidance of anyone who went astray is in putting forward his rationale and not the text revealed by Allah, and putting forward the following of desire and not the following of Allah's Commandment."[22] Ibn Taymiyah's writing is in itself mostly made up of quotations from the **Generous Qur'an** and *hadiths* of our **Prophet Muhammad** (*prayers and peace of* **ALLAH** *be upon him*).

The **Generous Qur'an** and man both have infinite dimensions. Their respective realities are parallel to each other and cannot be separated. The **Generous Qur'an** delineates the *Shari'atu* **ALLAH** (*subhanahu wa ta'ala*) (the Law of God). The *Shari'ah* helps man, especially the true believer, to live in congruence with the human essence and thereby to stay on the Straight Path. Thus, when any human being follows the teachings of the **Generous Qur'an**, as well as the practice of our **Prophet Muhammad** (*prayers and peace of* **ALLAH** *be upon him*), he is coming home to his very own essence. Through this practice he is remembering what is inside him. Thus, reality is not a source of perplexity, nor a puzzle which has to be deliberated over in order to be understood.

Our **Prophet Muhammad** (*prayers and peace of* **ALLAH** *be upon him*) has been given the analogy as being the embodiment of the **Generous Qur'an** in practice. In fact, he is described in certain *hadiths* as a "walking Qur'an". His *praxis* was therefore the Word

86

of **ALLAH** (*subhanahu wa ta'ala*) in application, and thus when humans follow his *Sunnah*, they are establishing the Word of **ALLAH** (*subhanahu wa ta'ala*) in their life. Muslims can hear the Word of **ALLAH** (*subhanahu wa ta'ala*) with their ears, see it with their eyes, speak it on their tongue, and also try to follow its teachings in all aspects of their lives. Thus, the Word which came upon the **Prophet Muhammad** (*prayers and peace of ALLAH be upon him*) as a reminder of the human essence is in itself the way to rediscover that essence. It is *from* the human essence as well as *for* it. Within it is the aggregation of all realms of being and the solution to the human predicament.[23] It constitutes the belief and the practice of Islam.

The Prophetic Decodification of the Word

To a Muslim believer, the **Generous Qur'an** is the way. The **Generous Qur'an** to him is void of puzzles or symbols. It is a simple Word that leads him to certainty. This is why it is distinguished from poetry, which is comprised of symbols and puzzles arising from the subjective perceptions of the poet.

87

****

<u>SURAH XXXVI (36)</u> *Ya Sin*

69. And We have not taught him (Muhammad) poetry, nor is it meet for him. This is naught else than a Reminder and a Lecture making plain.

وَمَا عَلَّمْنَاهُ الشِّعْرَ وَمَا يَنْبَغِي لَهُ اِنْ هُوَ اِلَّا ذِكْرٌ وَقُرْآنٌ مُبِينٌ ۝

XXXVI *Surah Ya Sin*, **The Generous Qur'an** 36:69

****

To most human beings, the **Generous Qur'an** contains an aggregation of symbols which could be understood at many levels. Our **Prophet Muhammad** (*prayers and peace of* **ALLAH** *be upon him*) alone, with the guidance of **ALLAH** (*subhanahu wa ta'ala*), was able to become conscious of the multiplicity of dimensions of the meaning of the **Generous Qur'an** at many levels.[24] These meanings are not separate but in actuality are integrated. As described above, the Messenger of **ALLAH** (*subhanahu wa ta'ala*) embodied the practice of the divine message. That is to say, his practice itself constituted the decodification of the verses of the **Generous Qur'an**.

According to the teaching of our **Prophet Muhammad** (*prayers and peace of* **ALLAH** *be upon him*), a Muslim true believer starts with the verse of the **Generous Qur'an** in Arabic. The proper place to start is not one's understanding of the world, but rather the

88

Word itself, in which is embedded the multiplicity of meaning, conception, application and being. After one starts with the verse, he goes from the verse to the realities that exist in the world. Then, from the multiplicity of existence and meaning, he goes back to the verse. This process continues through the course of his life to the point that he hears the **Qur'anic** verse inside creation and sees all of existence in the verse. Thus, the verse becomes the unity between the multiplicity of existent reality and the consciousness of the particular reader.

This unity flows throughout the **Generous Qur'an**, because it can only be explained through itself. This is why it is called "Generous". One conception of a word and its ideational ramifications in one verse are explained in another verse. Finally, the verse becomes the linkage between the particular and the universal. The pious reader finds refuge which spreads out in a generous dimension between the particular and the universal.[25]

The Function of Symbols in the Generous Qur'an

Islam holds that the **Generous Qur'an** has many levels of conceptual understanding. The first aspect of this understanding is that God's infinite consciousness is reflected in His infinite Word. Most human beings, when they read and understand the **Generous Qur'an**, are using their particular cognition. The latter is limited by human faculties which at best can only encompass a certain part of the spectrum of knowledge. In spite of these limited human faculties, God's words, as manifested in the **Generous Qur'an**, were sent to all human beings in the Arabic language in the anticipation

89

that humankind could find understanding, application, solution and meaning in the **Generous Qur'anic** verses. Accordingly, **ALLAH** (*subhanahu wa ta'ala*) was addressing all humankind at all levels of stratification. From the Islamic perspective, He wants humans to understand His Word at their human level of consciousness, whether or not they are Muslims. Thus the **Generous Qur'an** is seen as a mercy to all mankind.

****

SURAH XIV (14) *Abraham*

In the name of Allah, the Beneficent,
the Merciful.

1. Alif. Lam. Ra. (This is) a Scripture which We have revealed unto thee (Muhammad) that thereby thou mayst bring forth mankind from darkness unto light, by the permission of their Lord, unto the path of the Mighty, the Owner of Praise,

اياتها (١٤) سورة ابراهيم مكية ركوعاتها

بِسْمِ اللهِ الرَّحْمٰنِ الرَّحِيْمِ

الٓرٰ كِتٰبٌ اَنْزَلْنٰهُ اِلَيْكَ لِتُخْرِجَ النَّاسَ مِنَ الظُّلُمٰتِ اِلَى النُّوْرِ بِاِذْنِ رَبِّهِمْ اِلٰى صِرَاطِ الْعَزِيْزِ الْحَمِيْدِۙ١

XIV *Surah Ibrahim*, **The Generous Qur'an** 14:1

****

The Word of **ALLAH** (*subhanahu wa ta'ala*) could be understood by any human being. One's conception is contingent upon his faculties. As a result, each verse of the **Generous Qur'an** has many dimensions of conception. One dimension is the spatial

90

dimension. The spatial dimension implies a distance of consciousness between the speaker and the audience. Some members of this audience are ordinary Muslims, some are pious Muslims and some are non-Muslims. Some of the audience might not be in tune with the Path of Islam, and may not have made total surrender to the Lord. In this case, they do not know that they are *'abd* **ALLAH** (*subhanahu wa ta'ala*). Therefore, their distance from the Path of **ALLAH** (*subhanahu wa ta'ala*) has inhibited their understanding of a verse's meaning. For the pious true believer, however, every verse of the **Generous Qur'an** is a source of certainty and guidance, as is indicated in the first two verses of *Surah Baqqara:*

****

<u>SURAH II (2) *The Cow*</u>

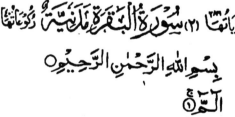

In the name of Allah, the Beneficent,
the Merciful.

1. Alif. Lam. Mim.

2. This is the Scripture wherein there is no doubt, a guidance unto those who ward off (evil):

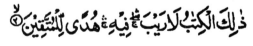

II *Surah Al-Baqqara*, **The Generous Qur'an** 2:1-2

****

91

Chapter III. The Generous Qur'an *Pari Passu* the Word of ALLAH

However, to a person who's consciousness is distant from the Path of **ALLAH** (*subhanahu wa ta'ala*), it becomes difficult to understand the meaning of the verses in this Book. From the Islamic perspective, that person who's consciousness is at a far distance from the Path of Islam has a series of veils and obstructions which distance him from the verse.[26] Whether or not he calls himself a Muslim is not really the issue. It is his human predicament that makes his consciousness to be at a far distance from the Path. A metaphor for this spatial distancing is the situation of a deaf person. If a person is speaking loudly to another person who is right beside him and who has ears but is deaf, the problem is not with the person who is speaking but with the deaf person. However close the deaf person comes, it makes no difference. He will not hear or understand unless his obstacle of deafness is overcome. The only way communication can be established with such a person is through the use of signs or symbols.

According to Islam, there are many such people in the world, with predicaments of many kinds. Many people thus can never understand the conceptual meaning (*'ibara*) of a simple sentence unless they go through a process of metamorphosis. To help them to solve these predicaments, **ALLAH** (*subhanahu wa ta'ala*) chose to give them symbolic meaning in the verse, in the anticipation that, through this symbolic meaning, they could overcome the spatial distance of their consciousness from the Path which prevents them from understanding the **Generous Qur'an**. These symbols are compatible with their cognition, making it easy for them to differentiate and recognize meanings. If they succeed in coming to an understanding, this would be a prelude to their following the

92

Chapter III. The Generous Qur'an *Pari Passu* the Word of ALLAH

Path of **ALLAH** (*subhanahu wa ta'ala*) and thus implementing His *Shari'ah*. They would see in the Word of **ALLAH** (*subhanahu wa ta'ala*) the perfect existence of the creation of **ALLAH** (*subhanahu wa ta'ala*). In that physical and metaphysical, spatial and non-spatial existence, they would see and understand the profound eloquence of each word, sign and symbol of the **Generous Qur'an**. They would take a trip from a far distance back to the Straight Path of **ALLAH** (*subhanahu wa ta'ala*).27 Signals and indicators could be in the macroscopic, infinite dimension of outer space, as well as in the microscopic dimensions imbedded within the human being. The verse in itself constitutes the linkage between the microscopic and the macroscopic dimensions which simultaneously asserts yet abolishes an infinite distance in the anticipation of crystallizing the infinite Power of **ALLAH** (*subhanahu wa ta'ala*). This in itself is a symbolic indicator of the mysterious realm of existence that **ALLAH** (*subhanahu wa ta'ala*) has created.

****

SURAH XLI (41) *Fusilat*

53. We shall show them Our portents on the horizons and within themselves until it will be manifest unto them that it is the Truth. Doth not thy Lord suffice, since He is Witness over all things?

سَنُرِيهِمْ ءَايَٰتِنَا فِى ٱلْءَافَاقِ وَفِىٓ أَنفُسِهِمْ حَتَّىٰ يَتَبَيَّنَ لَهُمْ أَنَّهُ ٱلْحَقُّ أَوَلَمْ يَكْفِ بِرَبِّكَ أَنَّهُ عَلَىٰ كُلِّ شَىْءٍ شَهِيدٌ ۝

XLI *Surah Al-Sajdah*, **The Generous Qur'an** 41:53

****

93

Chapter III. The Generous Qur'an *Pari Passu* the Word of ALLAH

According to this understanding, **ALLAH** (*subhanahu wa ta'ala*) uses symbolic meaning in the **Generous Qur'an** as a blessing, kindness and compassion, both to the one whose consciousness is close to the Path and the one whose consciousness is far from the Path. This is because the close and the far both have predicaments in various degrees, just as one person may be 100% deaf while another is 90% deaf. Both of these cannot fully distinguish sounds, and if a person wants to guide them, he has to take this predicament into consideration. Sound as a medium of communication becomes irrelevant for guiding them to their destination. As a result, one must mobilize other factors that the receiver's faculties can differentiate and use in decodifying the message. This is why in the **Generous Qur'an** there are infinite signs which are compatible with the variety of cognitions present throughout time. Some of these timeless signs had a particular meaning fourteen hundred years ago which became expanded in the age of modern science, when man is attempting to explore the physical universe in greater detail than ever before. The signs of **ALLAH** (*subhanahu wa ta'ala*) throughout the **Generous Qur'an**, as well as throughout the universe, from within its sub-atomic to beyond its astronomical realms, are inviting man to come to grips with the absolute reality of **ALLAH** (*subhanahu wa ta'ala*) which transcends the illusionary interplay between space and time.

This chapter has discussed various issues related to the **Generous Qur'an**, *pari passu*, the Word of **ALLAH** (*subhanahu wa ta'ala*), centering around the relationship of creation in general and humanity in particular to the Divine Word. The next chapter will explore these and other issues further, with special attention to the implications of the **Generous Qur'an's** exclusive status as the only authentic Word of **ALLAH** (*subhanahu wa ta'ala*).

94

Endnotes

[1]Harry Redner, "Representation and the Crisis of Post-Modernism", *PS* , (Summer, 1987), pp. 673-678.

[2]Anonymous, "Arcs: In the Beginning. . .", *Parabola,* (vol. 8, no. 3), pp. 66.

[3]Paul Ricoeur, "Naming God", *Union Seminary Quarterly Review,* (vol. 34, no. 4, Summer, 1979), p.227.

[4]W. Donald Hudson, "The Concept of Divine Transcendence", *Religious Studies,* (vol. 15, no. 2, June, 1979), p. 198.

[5]Ibid., pp.201-202.

[6]Ibid., pp.204-206.

[7]Bertel Wahlström, "The Relativity of Meaning", *Religious Studies,* (vol. 22, no. 2, June, 1986), pp. 205-209.

[8]Faqir Nur Muhammad Sarwari Qadri, *Irfan: A True and Unique Book of Divine Knowledge,* (Lahore, Pakistan: Ripon Printing Press. n.d.), pp. 45-59.

[9]Arberry, A.J. (translator), *The Discourses of Rumi,* (New York: Samuel Weiser, 1972), pp. 236-237.

[10]Charles Le Gai Eaton, *Islam and the Destiny of Man*, (Albany, New York: State University of New York Press/Islamic Texts Society, 1985), pp. 80-95.

[11]Muhammad Abul Quasem (translator), *The Jewels of the Qur'an: Al-Ghazali's Theory*, (London: Kegan Paul International, 1977, 1983), pp. 34-48.

[12]Faqir Nur Muhammad Sarwari Qadri, Op. Cit., pp. 219-227.

[13]Charles Le Gai Eaton, Op. Cit., pp. 92-95.

[14]Faqir Nur Muhammad Sarwari Qadri, Op. Cit., pp. 231-240.

[15]William Chittick, "The Words of the All-Merciful", *Parabola*, (vol. VIII, no. 3), pp. 18-20.

[16]Ibid., p. 19.

[17]Ibid., p. 23.

[18]Faqir Nur Muhammad Sarwari Qadri, Op. Cit., pp. 206-209.

[19]Seyyed Hossein Nasr, *Ideas and Realities of Islam*, (London: Allen & Unwin, 1966), pp. 50-66.

[20]Taqee Ad-Deen Ibn Taymiyah, *Al-'Uboodiyah: The Essay of Worship* (Elizabeth, New Jersey: Daar Al-Hadeeth, 1987), pp. 46-54.

[21]Faqir Nur Muhammad Sarwari Qadri, Op. Cit., pp. 33-45.

[22]Taqee Ad-Deen Ibn Taymiyah, Op. Cit., p. 46.

[23]Faqir Nur Muhammad Sarwari Qadri, Op. Cit., pp. 19-30.

[24]Bediuzzaman Said Nursi, *The Miracles of Muhammad: The Testimony of History*, (El Cerrito, California: Risale-i Nur Institute of America, 1976), pp. 111-129.

[25]Faqir Nur Muhammad Sarwari Qadri, Op. Cit., pp. 127-135.

[26]Ibid., pp. 129-141.

[27]Sheikh Muzaffer Ozak Al-Jerrahi, *The Unveiling of Love: Sufism and the Remembrance of God*, (New York: Inner Traditions International, 1981), pp.99-115.

CHAPTER IV

The Generous Qur'an as the Only Authentic Word of ALLAH

Qur'anic Revelation in Islam

Truth does not need to be defended. It survives regardless of any obstacles, including the illusionary interplay between space and time. The Word of **ALLAH** (*subhanahu wa ta'ala*) is the Way, the Truth and the Light. It is contained, allegorically, empirically, contextually, profoundly, eloquently and infinitely in the **Generous Qur'an**. The latter in itself thus becomes the Way, the Truth and the Light. The proof of this is that it has survived without being modified, rearticulated or reconceptualized to fit the changing variables of the human condition. Our Arabian **Prophet Muhammad** (*prayers and peace of* **ALLAH** *be upon him*) is the **Generous Qur'an** in practice, the completion and the Seal of the Way, the Truth and the Light. Though Jesus (*peace be upon him*) came to fulfill the Word, our beloved Arabian **Prophet Muhammad** (*prayers and peace of* **ALLAH** *be upon him*) came to complete it.

The Truth shines with Light that no obstacle can stop. Thereby, it is auto-legitimating. Its straightness, without any crookedness, is an indication of its divine origin and preservation. Its jewels and pearls reveal themselves and crystallize their light.

98

As a result, **ALLAH** (*subhanahu wa ta'ala*) has established His Word and the *Din* (Way, religion) of Islam in the whole Spaceship Earth, as well as the rest of the universe, as the abiding force of the human melodrama. The Way, the Truth and the Light came in the revelation that came through the beloved Arabian **Prophet Muhammad** (*prayers and peace of* **ALLAH** *be upon him*). Thus, our Arabian Prophet, the beloved one (*prayers and peace of* **ALLAH** *be upon him*) became the World-Light-Splendor. **ALLAH** (*subhanahu wa ta'ala*) has fulfilled His promise that He will continuously establish Islam on the Spaceship Earth and throughout the whole universe, and no force can challenge the order of **ALLAH** (*subhanahu wa ta'ala*) in His domain. Thereby, though this revelation descended on the **Prophet Muhammad** (*prayers and peace of* **ALLAH** *be upon him*) it existed prior to creation and will continue unto eternity. The Way revealed to the World-Light-Splendor is the first and the last way. This is authentic Islam, submission to the Lord.

The **Generous Qur'an** is the actual, authentic and indisputable Word of God (Who calls Himself **ALLAH** (*subhanahu wa ta'ala*)). **ALLAH** (*subhanahu wa ta'ala*) has committed Himself to protecting the **Generous Qur'an** and making it immune from alteration or change. Since the time it was revealed until today, it is still in its original, authentic and autonomous form. Not one letter, accent, word or punctuation mark has been added or subtracted. Therefore, any comparison between the **Generous Qur'an** and any other book or proclaimed scripture in the world, such as the New and Old Testaments, is irrelevant and incommensurable, and lacks the semblance of legitimacy. There is a diametrical and infinite difference between when **ALLAH** (*subhanahu wa ta'ala*),

Chapter IV. The Generous Qur'an as the Only Authentic Word of ALLAH

generously and explicitly reveals reality, with jewel- and pearl-like certainty and infinite Light, in the **Generous Qur'an,** and when man hypothesizes, guesses and speculates in the historical Bible in the name of God. The historical Bible is distinct from the original, authentic, verbatim Word of God, including the tablets of the Torah, *pari passu*, the *Taurat* , the Gospel, *pari passu* the*Injeel*, and the Psalms, *pari passu* the *Zabur*. The latter no longer exist *in toto*. **ALLAH** (*subhanahu wa ta'ala*) wanted it this way. This does not mean that the authentic Word of **ALLAH** (*subhanahu wa ta'ala*) could ever decay, unless His order comes, because His Word *is* creation itself. His Word never decays or disintegrates, because He preserves it. It is man's hypotheses, guesses, speculations and writings that decay and wither away, proving to be, in retrospect, void of a real meaning. This is because of the limitations of man. Man's consciousness can never encompass God's consciousness. Thus the self-styled Jewish writer Paul of Tarsus, who wrote parts of what became the Christian Bible, as well as those who wrote the canonical gospels now in the Bible, cannot encompass God's consciousness. They are encapsulated within the illusionary interplay between space and time, though some of their concepts have limited meaning, which is thereby not authentic. The **Generous Qur'an**, in its entirety can be contained in the chest of individual Muslims who memorize it. One rarely or never hears, by contrast, of a person memorizing the Bible.

The first words of the **Generous Qur'an** to be revealed to the Arab **Prophet Muhammad** (*prayers and peace of* **ALLAH** *be upon him*) were (in a rough interpretation in English) *"Recite! In the Name of your Lord"*. In this final decent of Absolute Revelation, the Word did not become flesh, which is fleeting, but stayed as a

100

Chapter IV. The Generous Qur'an as the Only Authentic Word of ALLAH

Word which could be recited, remembered and held forever in the hearts of the believers. The **Prophet Muhammad** (*prayers and peace of* **ALLAH** *be upon him*) became the beloved and pure receptacle and transmitter of the Word. **ALLAH** (*subhanahu wa ta'ala*) deliberately appointed an unlettered Prophet to be the receptacle of His Divine Message in order to separate the holy contents of the Word from human acquired knowledge.[1] The **Prophet Muhammad** (*prayers and peace of* **ALLAH** *be upon him*) was therefore a purely passive receptacle for the unadulterated transmission of the Word as it was revealed, without human interference. The Arabic language in which the **Generous Qur'an** was revealed therefore takes on a sacrosanctity for the believer, who by reciting and reading the Book of **ALLAH** (*subhanahu wa ta'ala*) participates in the 'Divine Presence'. Knowing Arabic is therefore an imperative variable in the infinite structural equation of a Muslim's understanding of the **Generous Qur'an**.[2]

The **Generous Qur'an** is the source of all knowledge. In this respect it is *Umm Al-Kitab* (The Mother of the Book). This knowledge is expressed in its eloquent terminology which is sometimes explicit and sometimes cryptically concealed. The seeds and principles of all information and knowledge are expressed in it. One may find the principles of metaphysics, religion, and cosmology, as well as all of the social, juridical, biological, physical, technological and medical sciences, in the **Generous Qur'an**. The principles expounded in the **Generous Qur'an** are eternal truths. The **Generous Qur'an** is never outdated. Even its stories of the fate of ancient peoples and civilizations tell us of abiding principles and characteristics of human weakness and strength, and the certain recompense which is dealt to humanity as reward or punishment.

101

Chapter IV. The Generous Qur'an as the Only Authentic Word of ALLAH

These are perennial accounts of the recurrent expression of the human condition. It is a revealed Book for all times, and is the ultimate guide.

Revelation (*wahi*) has been defined by the contemporary scholar Yaqub Zaki as "the act by which God, having created this world, proceeds to disclose Himself to His own creation, acting in His capacity as *hadi* (Guide)".[3] Revelation may come in many forms and through many intermediaries or through certain lineages. It may be written, such as is the case with the **Generous Qur'an**, or it may be oral, such as the *hadith*. **ALLAH** (*subhanahu wa ta'ala*) has chosen to send revelations through the medium of human beings by selecting certain prophets, who are of exceptional qualities, to deliver the message directly to other humans.

The decent of the revelation in the **Generous Qur'an** comes directly from **ALLAH** (*subhanahu wa ta'ala*). The term *anzala* means that **ALLAH** (*subhanahu wa ta'ala*) *sent down* something which was already in existence with Him. The **Generous Qur'an**, in other words, has an eternal, *a priori* presence that transcends space and time, and exists with **ALLAH** (*subhanahu wa ta'ala*).[4] **ALLAH** (*subhanahu wa ta'ala*) confirms the infallibility of the **Generous Qur'an** by describing it as deriving from the *lauh al-mahfuth* meaning a "preserved (or guarded) tablet". **ALLAH** (*subhanahu wa ta'ala*) is the One who guards, has guarded and will continue to guard the authenticity of the **Generous Qur'an** against any alteration or corruption.

102

****

<u>SURAH LXXXV (85)</u> *The Mansions*
of the Stars

21. Nay, but it is a glorious Qur'an.

22. On a guarded tablet.

بَلْ هُوَ قُرْآنٌ مَجِيدٌ ۞
فِى لَوْحٍ مَحْفُوظٍ ۞

LXXXV *Surah Al-Buruj,* **The Generous Qur'an** 85:21-22

****

Given that the **Generous Qur'an** is an infallible textual revelation from **ALLAH** (*subhanahu wa ta'ala*), one finds that it serves as an inimitable, unquestionable cornerstone of authority for the community of believers who seek guidance. As such, the **Generous Qur'an** provides the linkage which bridges the hierarchical gap between human society and **ALLAH** (*subhanahu wa ta'ala*). The **Generous Qur'an** provides the ultimate tangible and readable guidelines for man's socio-political organization. In this respect, it brings the metaphysical message of Islam to a lower, socio-political realm where humans may find direct applicability and relevance to human mundane and spiritual affairs. The society of believers and non-believers may be organized around its precepts.[5] It is the vehicle of communication between the higher and lower planes. As such, the Muslim's socio-political organization can never take on an independence and supremacy of

103

its own.   Human organization must recognize the hierarchical ordering of the Word which derives from **ALLAH** (*subhanahu wa ta'ala*).   That is why the Word must be kept and understood in Arabic, for it maintains its divine linkage as the Word of **ALLAH** (*subhanahu wa ta'ala*).   To use "translations" in other languages as the ultimate authority for guiding socio-political organization would be to break the linkage between higher and lower planes and attempt to legitimize and institute man-made interpretations as divine.   As the self-styled Christians and Jews know, the mechanism of translation can be used as a tool with which to redirect the words of **ALLAH** (*subhanahu wa ta'ala*) towards certain temporally approved channels.   But because the **Generous Qur'an** remains intact, it holds a superiority in its originality over interpretations.

Reason and Revelation in the Generous Qur'an

Revelation, while it is associated with divine ordinances that are of an unquestionable nature, is not an exclusively non-rational phenomenon in Islam.[6]   The classical distinction between rationality and revelation was made to distinguish between the origin of the two kinds of knowledge.   Abstract theoretical reasoning can be carried out systematically to provide theoretically and apparently "convincing" conclusions that are not derived from absolute divine ordinances.   Theories can be built upon the resulting philosophical conclusions and can be used to direct human behavior in the presence or absence of religion.

Chapter IV. The Generous Qur'an as the Only Authentic Word of ALLAH

Reason can be isolated from revelation, but revelation does not necessarily have to be isolated from reason. In Islam, the revelations of **ALLAH** (*subhanahu wa ta'ala*) in the **Generous Qur'an** often call upon productive human reasoning to further convince us that our faith in the revelation is truthful. On various topics, **ALLAH** (*subhanahu wa ta'ala*) gives us reasons why we should believe in the truthfulness of His assertions. For example, **ALLAH** (*subhanahu wa ta'ala*) gives many reasons why He is the One and Only God, why we should even believe that **ALLAH** (*subhanahu wa ta'ala*) exists, why we should believe in life after death, why we should pray to and obey **ALLAH** (*subhanahu wa ta'ala*), and why we should worship **ALLAH** (*subhanahu wa ta'ala*).[7]

There are many reasonable examples that **ALLAH** (*subhanahu wa ta'ala*) gives to help humans back up their faith in the unseen. For example, **ALLAH** (*subhanahu wa ta'ala*) tells us why we should believe that Jesus Christ (*peace be upon him*) is a prophet of **ALLAH** (*subhanahu wa ta'ala*) and not the son of **ALLAH** (*subhanahu wa ta'ala*). **ALLAH** (*subhanahu wa ta'ala*) asserts that the miraculous virgin birth of Jesus (*peace be upon him*) does not necessarily lead to the conclusion that **ALLAH** (*subhanahu wa ta'ala*) begot a son. **ALLAH** (*subhanahu wa ta'ala*) continues by saying that if we only think about how **ALLAH** (*subhanahu wa ta'ala*) created Adam (*peace be upon him*) out of nothing, we can then reason that it is not a hard or unusual task for **ALLAH** (*subhanahu wa ta'ala*) to put Jesus (*peace be upon him*) in the womb of a virgin at the command of His omnipotent Word and order.

* *

SURAH III (3) *The Family of 'Imran*

59.   Lo! The likeness of Jesus with Allah is as the likeness of Adam. He created him of dust, then He said unto him: Be! and he is.

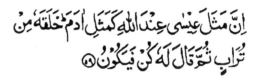

III *Surah Ali-'Imran*, **The Generous Qur'an** 3:59

* *

By giving us this metaphor about Adam and Jesus (*peace be upon them*) to ponder, **ALLAH** (*subhanahu wa ta'ala*) is pointing out to humans that the creation of Jesus (*peace be upon him*) is no more miraculous than the creation of Adam (*peace be upon him*). Reasoning would then lead us to conclude that the formation of Jesus (*peace be upon him*) in the womb is not such a difficult task when compared to the formation of original man out of nothingness. In the final analysis, both forms of creation are easy for **ALLAH** (*subhanahu wa ta'ala*), who has only to say to something "Be" and it is (*kun fa yakun*). One does not, therefore, have to look at Jesus' (*peace be upon him*) virgin birth and conclude that **ALLAH** (*subhanahu wa ta'ala*) must be "the father" or that Jesus (*peace be upon him*) would have to be a "son" of **ALLAH** (*subhanahu wa ta'ala*) by any necessity.

By giving us this analysis to ponder, **ALLAH** (*subhanahu wa ta'ala*) is further encouraging humans to use their minds to confirm

106

their beliefs. Faith, however, in all cases comes first.[8] When **ALLAH** (*subhanahu wa ta'ala*) tells us that Jesus (*peace be upon him*) is a prophet with the Holy Spirit and not the son of **ALLAH** (*subhanahu wa ta'ala*), a true Muslim believes this without any doubt, question or need for rational proof. This is the nature of revelation: it is absolute and its acceptance is unequivocal and unquestionable. However, for those whose faith is weak or who just enjoy rational discourse, **ALLAH** (*subhanahu wa ta'ala*) gives rational evidence that one might ponder in order to arrive at the same divinely revealed conclusion.

Human reasoning is not barred from the range of acceptable activities for the believers in Islam. While faith requires one to believe without question, a proper form of reasoning and reflection is, in fact, encouraged in Islam. Improper forms of reason are condemned in the **Generous Qur'an**, as **ALLAH** (*subhanahu wa ta'ala*) seeks to eliminate undue reliance upon false or quasi reason that is influenced by *Shaytan* (Satan). Such *Shaytanic* forms of human rationality do not lead us to a better understanding of the truth, but rather serve to hinder us by setting up rationally contrived barriers which serve as veils that prevent us from seeing the Light of Truth.[9]

ALLAH (*subhanahu wa ta'ala*) forbids the use of conjecture and speculation (*thann*, in Arabic) as a substitute for truth. Conjecture is based upon uncertainty and mere speculation and is not a reliable source of truth. **ALLAH** (*subhanahu wa ta'ala*) also discredits the dependence upon mere whim (*hawa*) as also unreliable in discerning the truth, for it adds a mixture of irrational desires and passions which distorts the truth. **ALLAH** (*subhanahu wa ta'ala*) asserts:

107

****

<u>SURAH IV (4)</u> *Women*

135. O ye who believe! Be staunch in justice, witnesses for Allah, even though it be against yourselves or (your) parents or (your) kindred, whether (the case be of) a rich or a poor man, for Allah is nearer unto both (than ye are). So follow not passion lest ye lapse (from truth) and if ye lapse or fall away, then lo! Allah is ever Informed of what ye do.

يَٰٓأَيُّهَا ٱلَّذِينَ ءَامَنُوا۟ كُونُوا۟ قَوَّٰمِينَ بِٱلْقِسْطِ شُهَدَآءَ لِلَّهِ وَلَوْ عَلَىٰٓ أَنفُسِكُمْ أَوِ ٱلْوَٰلِدَيْنِ وَٱلْأَقْرَبِينَ‌ۚ إِن يَكُنْ غَنِيًّا أَوْ فَقِيرًا فَٱللَّهُ أَوْلَىٰ بِهِمَا‌ۖ فَلَا تَتَّبِعُوا۟ ٱلْهَوَىٰٓ أَن تَعْدِلُوا۟‌ۚ وَإِن تَلْوُۥٓا۟ أَوْ تُعْرِضُوا۟ فَإِنَّ ٱللَّهَ كَانَ بِمَا تَعْمَلُونَ خَبِيرًا ۝

IV *Surah Al-Nisaa,* **The Generous Qur'an** 4:135

****

Not only does **ALLAH** (*subhanahu wa ta'ala*) condemn improper reasoning, but He also condemns those who are unable to reason at all and who lack faith as well. In this respect He condemns the blind imitation of the practices, worships and beliefs of established (yet illegitimate) authority such as cultural customs, ancestors, parents and traditions, etc., This is known as *taqlid al-a'ma* (blind imitation).

108

****

SURAH V (5) *The Table Spread*

104. And when it is said unto them:
Come unto that which Allah hath
revealed and unto the messenger, they
say: Enough for us is that wherein we
found our fathers. What! even
though their fathers had no
knowledge whatsoever, and no
guidance?

وَإِذَا قِيلَ لَهُمْ تَعَالَوْا إِلَى مَا أَنْزَلَ اللهُ وَإِلَى
الرَّسُولِ قَالُوا حَسْبُنَا مَا وَجَدْنَا عَلَيْهِ آبَاءَنَا أَوَلَوْ
كَانَ آبَاؤُهُمْ لَا يَعْلَمُونَ شَيْئًا وَلَا يَهْتَدُونَ ۝

V *Surah Al-Ma'ida,* **The Generous Qur'an** 5:104

****

Coercion (*ikrah*) is also excluded as a method of establishing
belief. **ALLAH** (*subhanahu wa ta'ala*) acknowledges that one
cannot be compelled to believe under any circumstances. **ALLAH**
(*subhanahu wa ta'ala*) says:

* *

SURAH II (2) *The Cow*

256.   There is no compulsion in religion.   The right direction is henceforth distinct from error. And he who rejecteth false deities and believeth in Allah hath grasped a firm handhold which will never break. Allah is Hearer, Knower.

لَآ إِكْرَاهَ فِى الدِّينِ قَد تَّبَيَّنَ الرُّشْدُ مِنَ الْغَيِّ فَمَن يَكْفُرْ بِالطَّاغُوتِ وَيُؤْمِنۢ بِاللَّهِ فَقَدِ اسْتَمْسَكَ بِالْعُرْوَةِ الْوُثْقَىٰ لَا انفِصَامَ لَهَا وَاللَّهُ سَمِيعٌ عَلِيمٌ ۝

II *Surah Al-Baqqara*, **The Generous Qur'an 2:256**

* *

Because the truth is apparent, faith and proper reasoning are sufficient to ascertain Truth without recourse to coercion or compulsion.

ALLAH (*subhanahu wa ta'ala*) furthermore forbids humans from relying upon magical superstition as a substitute for truth. Irrational superstitions, especially black magic, can corrupt the purity, simplicity and proximity of the truth, since they distort it and mix it in with hidden forces which are often evil.

110

* *

SURAH II (2) *The Cow*

102.   ...And follow that which the devils falsely related against the kingdom of Solomon. Solomon disbelieved not; but the devils disbelieved, teaching mankind magic and that which was revealed to the two angels in Babel, Harut and Marut. Nor did they (the two angels) teach it to anyone till they had said: We are only a temptation, therefore disbelieve not (in the guidance of Allah). And from these two (angels) people learn that by which they cause division between man and wife; but they injure thereby no-one save by Allah's leave. And they learn that which harmeth them and profiteth them not. And surely they do know that he who trafficketh therein will have no (happy) portion in the Hereafter; and surely evil is the price for which they sell their souls, if they but knew.

II *Surah Al-Baqqara*, **The Generous Qur'an** 2:102

* *

111

Chapter IV. The Generous Qur'an as the Only Authentic Word of ALLAH

Finally, human faith and reason should not be thwarted by undue reliance upon or belief in the opinions and decrees of some sort of clergy. **ALLAH** (*subhanahu wa ta'ala*) asserts that believing individuals each have access to knowledge of **ALLAH** (*subhanahu wa ta'ala*) and the truth if they have *taqwa*, meaning piety. In other words, it is the level of piety in the heart that opens the doors to truth. In the past and present, undue reliance upon a clerical class led to a form of false worship of those people who claimed to have exclusive access to the truth. In fact, many pious believers were misled by these clerics, monks and rabbis who abused their authority and set themselves and their decrees and rulings between **ALLAH** (*subhanahu wa ta'ala*) and mankind.

112

Chapter IV. The Generous Qur'an as the Only Authentic Word of ALLAH

****

SURAH IX (9) *Repentance*

31. They have taken as lords beside Allah their rabbis and their monks and the Messiah son of Mary, when they were bidden to worship only One God. There is no god save Him. Be He glorified from all that they ascribe as partner (unto Him)!

اِتَّخَذُوٓا اَحْبَارَهُمْ وَرُهْبَانَهُمْ اَرْبَابًا مِّن دُونِ اللهِ وَالْمَسِيحَ ابْنَ مَرْيَمَ وَمَآ اُمِرُوٓا اِلَّا لِيَعْبُدُوٓا اِلٰهًا وَاحِدًا لَّآ اِلٰهَ اِلَّا هُوَ سُبْحَانَهُ عَمَّا يُشْرِكُونَ ۝

32. Fain would they put out the light of Allah with their mouths, but Allah disdaineth (aught) save that He shall perfect His light, however much the disbelievers are averse.

يُرِيدُونَ اَن يُطْفِئُوا نُورَ اللهِ بِاَفْوَاهِهِمْ وَيَاْبَى اللهُ اِلَّآ اَن يُتِمَّ نُورَهُ وَلَوْ كَرِهَ الْكَافِرُونَ ۝

IX *Surah Al-Tauba,* **The Generous Qur'an** 9:31-32

****

Once all these previously mentioned irrational, speculative, encapsulated and obstructed modes of obtaining knowledge are controlled or eliminated altogether, one may proceed to think, reason and reflect upon the Order of Things in all its manifestations: internal and external, hidden and revealed, written and perceived. The **Generous Qur'an** is one of the main focal points for one's reflection upon the Order of Things.

113

✱✱✱

SURAH XXXVIII (38) *Sad*

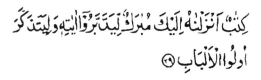

29. (This is) a Scripture that We
have revealed unto thee, full of
blessing, that they may ponder its
revelations, and that men of
understanding may reflect.

XXXVIII *Surah Sad*, **The Generous Qur'an** 38:29

✱✱✱

The **Generous Qur'an** contains all knowledge and is itself an
excellent source for reflection and thought.

There are different kinds of methods of reasoning which
ALLAH (*subhanahu wa ta'ala*) puts forth in the **Generous Qur'an**.
These are means or approaches by which our reason may lead us to
knowledge of the truth. One method is that **ALLAH** (*subhanahu
wa ta'ala*) refers to the truthfulness of something based upon its
being self-evident. **ALLAH** (*subhanahu wa ta'ala*) puts forth that it
is self-evident that **ALLAH** (*subhanahu wa ta'ala*) can only be One
due to the inherent harmony in the universe. In other words, the
reasoning goes that if there were more than one God there would be
chaos in the universe. This is a reflection which is self-evident.

114

****

SURAH XXI (21) *The Prophets*

22. If there were therein Gods beside Allah, then verily both (the heavens and the earth) had been disordered. Glorified be Allah, the Lord of the Throne, from all that they ascribe (unto Him).

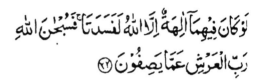

XXI *Surah Al-Anbiya'*, **The Generous Qur'an** 21:22

****

In other cases, **ALLAH** (*subhanahu wa ta'ala*) details the order of His creation and asks humans if they cannot indeed confirm this perfection through their observation and sensory perception. In other words, **ALLAH** (*subhanahu wa ta'ala*) asserts that one has only to look at such things as the miracle of birth, or the growth of green plants from seeds, the transformation from death to life, the separation of salt and fresh water, the abundance of fresh edible fruits and vegetables, the servitude of domestic animals to man, etc., to see that **ALLAH** (*subhanahu wa ta'ala*) is the source of all life and death, contentment and disaster, etc. This observation can be a form of reason that leads to faith in **ALLAH** (*subhanahu wa ta'ala*). We do not have to rely on blind faith, in other words, because the visible evidence is compelling and plentiful.

115

＊＊＊

SURAH X (10) *Jonah*

101. Say: Behold what is in the heavens and the earth! But revelations and warnings avail not folk who will not believe.

قُلِ انْظُرُوا مَاذَا فِى السَّمَوَٰتِ وَالْأَرْضِ وَمَا تُغْنِى الْآيَٰتُ وَالنُّذُرُ عَن قَوْمٍ لَّا يُؤْمِنُونَ ۝

X *Surah Yunus*, **The Generous Qur'an** 10:101

＊＊＊

In addition to observation, **ALLAH** (*subhanahu wa ta'ala*) asks us to recall our direct experiences to provide additional reasonable proof of the presence and majesty of **ALLAH** (*subhanahu wa ta'ala*). Often humans, in the midst of crises or in a moment of weakness, instinctively turn to **ALLAH** (*subhanahu wa ta'ala*) to save them from sudden death or tragedy. The reasoning here is that if one's gut feelings in the midst of need confirm that there is a saving Grace, how then could one rationally deny **ALLAH** (*subhanahu wa ta'ala*) in good times? One's own experience of urgency is all that is necessary sometimes to confirm one's faith in **ALLAH** (*subhanahu wa ta'ala*). The only problem with this method of reasoning is that one soon lapses into indifference again when the crisis is relieved.

116

* *

SURAH X (10) *Jonah*

22. He it is Who maketh you to go on the land and sea till, when ye are in the ships and they sail with them with a fair breeze and they are glad therein, a storm-wind reacheth them and the wave cometh unto them from every side and they deem that they are overwhelmed therein; (then) they cry unto Allah, making their faith pure for Him only: If thou deliver us from this, we truly will be of the thankful.

23. Yet when He hath delivered them, behold! they rebel in the earth wrongfully. O mankind! Your rebellion is only against yourselves. (Ye have) enjoyment of the life of the world: then unto Us is your return and We shall proclaim unto you what ye used to do.

هُوَالَّذِى يُسَيِّرُكُمْ فِى الْبَرِّ وَالْبَحْرِ حَتَّى إِذَا كُنْتُمْ فِى الْفُلْكِ وَجَرَيْنَ بِهِمْ بِرِيحٍ طَيِّبَةٍ وَفَرِحُوا بِهَا جَاءَتْهَا رِيحٌ عَاصِفٌ وَجَاءَهُمُ الْمَوْجُ مِنْ كُلِّ مَكَانٍ وَظَنُّوا أَنَّهُمْ أُحِيطَ بِهِمْ دَعَوُا اللَّهَ مُخْلِصِينَ لَهُ الدِّينَ لَئِنْ أَنْجَيْتَنَا مِنْ هَذِهِ لَنَكُونَنَّ مِنَ الشَّاكِرِينَ ٢٢

فَلَمَّا أَنْجَاهُمْ إِذَا هُمْ يَبْغُونَ فِى الْأَرْضِ بِغَيْرِ الْحَقِّ يَا أَيُّهَا النَّاسُ إِنَّمَا بَغْيُكُمْ عَلَى أَنْفُسِكُمْ مَتَاعَ الْحَيَاةِ الدُّنْيَا ثُمَّ إِلَيْنَا مَرْجِعُكُمْ فَنُنَبِّئُكُمْ بِمَا كُنْتُمْ تَعْمَلُونَ ٢٣

X *Surah Yunus*, **The Generous Qur'an** 10:22-23

* *

Ultimately, it is better for the weak at heart to develop a long-term faith in **ALLAH** (*subhanahu wa ta'ala*) that could withstand the test of their experiences.

Another method of reason that **ALLAH** (*subhanahu wa ta'ala*) refers to in the **Generous Qur'an** is the appeal to the general interest of humanity (referred to in Arabic as *maslaha*). In some instances, **ALLAH** (*subhanahu wa ta'ala*) exhorts mankind to perform certain individual or collective obligations or to refrain from certain behavior because it is in the best interest of society in general and individuals in particular. **ALLAH** (*subhanahu wa ta'ala*) does not need to explain why humans should or should not do certain things. It is understood that what **ALLAH** (*subhanahu wa ta'ala*) makes lawful is good for humans and what He forbids is not.[10] The reason for the prohibition of the consumption of certain substances like alcohol and pork are self-evident. Alcohol consumption is known to destroy individuals' lives and families. Pork, on the other hand, contains a great deal of ureaic acid which is a toxin to the human body. While the modern trend in *kufur* society is to "cure" pork meat before it is eaten, **ALLAH's** (*subhanahu wa ta'ala*) blanket order to avoid the consumption of pork altogether is the best protection against its potential contaminants and resultant illness. Clearly, it is in the interest of people to avoid what **ALLAH** (*subhanahu wa ta'ala*) has prohibited.

Ultimately **ALLAH** (*subhanahu wa ta'ala*) exhorts people to do or not to do things, not just for their own interest in this mundane world, but for their interest in gaining the pleasures and the comforts of the next life. Man's faith in **ALLAH** (*subhanahu wa ta'ala*) and decision to believe in the Word and message of **ALLAH** (*subhanahu wa ta'ala*) is ultimately for man's own benefit in that

118

he will have achieved the fruits of his purpose on earth. Towards this direction, **ALLAH** (*subhanahu wa ta'ala*) encourages people to fulfill their responsibilities, by offering them detailed descriptions of the pleasures and gains in Heaven and the torment of punishment in Hell. Even a person of great faith could reason to himself that he would be better off observing the Laws of **ALLAH** (*subhanahu wa ta'ala*) if he wants to find ultimate peace.[11]

****

SURAH X (10) *Jonah*

108. Say: O mankind! Now hath the Truth from your Lord come unto you. So whosoever is guided, is guided only for (the good of) his soul, and whosoever erreth, erreth only against it. And I am not a warder over you.

قُلْ يَٰٓأَيُّهَا ٱلنَّاسُ قَدْ جَآءَكُمُ ٱلْحَقُّ مِن رَّبِّكُمْ فَمَنِ ٱهْتَدَىٰ فَإِنَّمَا يَهْتَدِى لِنَفْسِهِۦ وَمَن ضَلَّ فَإِنَّمَا يَضِلُّ عَلَيْهَا وَمَآ أَنَا۠ عَلَيْكُم بِوَكِيلٍ ۝

X *Surah Yunus*, **The Generous Qur'an** 10:108

****

Not only does **ALLAH** (*subhanahu wa ta'ala*) appeal to man's reason, senses, experiences, observations and interest, but also to his conscience whereby **ALLAH** (*subhanahu wa ta'ala*) makes the wrongdoers feel guilty for the crimes they commit against **ALLAH**

119

(*subhanahu wa ta'ala*) and other humans. **ALLAH** (*subhanahu wa ta'ala*) appeals to our inner conscience in this respect.

In all these instances, the reasoning described is directly linked to faith in **ALLAH** (*subhanahu wa ta'ala*) and His revelations. This reasoning merely serves to confirm the revelation. It is not abstract thinking. This means the divine ordinances, revelation and presence cannot be deduced purely by the process of abstract thinking alone, as some *kufur* "naturalists" assert. But, instead, **ALLAH** (*subhanahu wa ta'ala*) encourages human reasoning and reflection to enhance one's knowledge of the divine essence which created all that is apparent and hidden to him. Discoveries of Truth cannot be made in a religious void.[12] The secular rationalist does not have the tools to lead him to knowledge of the real truth.

The Myriad of Meanings

ALLAH (*subhanahu wa ta'ala*) promised to protect the **Generous Qur'an**, and He did fulfill His promise. **ALLAH** (*subhanahu wa ta'ala*), however, did not make such a promise regarding the Old or New Testament (*Taurat* or *Injeel*). There is not one divinely-revealed book in the world which has ever survived in its ultimate authenticity, language and applicability like the **Generous Qur'an**. There is only one book in the world which has crystallized its purity and dynamism to the final detail, and that is the **Generous Qur'an**. It has to be read in Arabic. When it is translated into any language other than Arabic, it is not the

120

Generous Qur'an anymore because it has been reduced by the limitations of human cognition and perceptions.

Only the **Generous Qur'an** in the Arabic language could explain any particular phenomenon to the final detail. English, French, German or any other language could not be the proper instrument to describe the Almighty phenomenon. The *shahada* (statement of "witness" through which the individual rectifies him- or herself to Islam): *la ilaha illa ALLAH, Muhammad rasul ALLAH* ("There is no god except ALLAH, and Muhammad is His Messenger") is a full, informative sentence without a verb. One could not translate this sentence verbatim or conceptually into any other language without inserting a verb. One would tend to say that *"there is no god except ALLAH"*, or *"nothing is except ALLAH"* as a translation for *la ilaha illa ALLAH*. Regardless of how a person translates this sentence, he is confined by the structural formation of his language, which in most cases requires the use of a verb. Therefore, one would be reducing the omnipotent to a time dimension expressed in the present tense. However, something that exists in a time dimension must have a beginning and an end. Thus, through the process of translation, the structural formations of non-Arabic languages contribute certain attributes and time references which the original meaning transcends.

Time is no more than an analytical, relativistic concept and a measurement of space and speed. If space does not exist with certainty, this means that time does not exist with certainty. Space and time contribute to the structural formation of a language. In some languages time is unilinear, thus explicitly implying that it has a beginning and an end. Therefore, using a time-bound terminology to describe **ALLAH** (*subhanahu wa ta'ala*) and His

121

Chapter IV. The Generous Qur'an as the Only Authentic Word of ALLAH

Word presents irreconcilable methodological adversities, and also reduces the true meaning of **ALLAH's** (*subhanahu wa ta'ala*) Word to something that it is not. **ALLAH's** (*subhanahu wa ta'ala*) Word, in Arabic, constantly abolishes the classical distinction between past, present and future. In many instances **ALLAH** (*subhanahu wa ta'ala*) uses a past tense verb which has implications for ex-post history, while at the same time describing a phenomenon in the continuous present.[13] The understanding of the issue becomes contingent upon the reader because, in the final analysis, from **ALLAH's** (*subhanahu wa ta'ala*) perspective everything is *fait accompli*. The understanding of any particular phenomenon is not bound with the present, past and future typology but with the level of consciousness that **ALLAH** (*subhanahu wa ta'ala*) reveals to the individual. The contextual ramification of that consciousness is contingent upon how many veils **ALLAH** (*subhanahu wa ta'ala*) will remove from the individual in order to allow the latter to see something which is already there. An individual is in reality not going back and forth in time. In actuality, **ALLAH** (*subhanahu wa ta'ala*) is just removing the veils from him to allow him to see something which has been there all along. Only **ALLAH** (*subhanahu wa ta'ala*) could articulate that particular phenomenon in simplistic and eloquent terminology, with straightness, openness and frankness, and without any crookedness.

The Arabic words of the **Generous Qur'an** are so simple and eloquent, yet because they come from the Almighty, each word or letter has imbedded in it an infinite number of meanings which human consciousness cannot fathom. When a human contemplates not only the words but each letter, as well as the pauses for breath, a new, infinite world of real existence and

122

Chapter IV. The Generous Qur'an as the Only Authentic Word of ALLAH

meaning opens up and becomes an independent reality to the point that human consciousness becomes stunned by the meticulous conception and articulation of **ALLAH** (*subhanahu wa ta'ala*). One realizes that the only thing that human consciousness can do is to make total submission and transform from the realm of understanding to the realm of prostration and believing "blindly", in a state of joy, thanking **ALLAH** (*subhanahu wa ta'ala*) that He made one a pious Muslim just to appreciate and find guidance in that Word.

An example of the infinite and unfathomable dimension of meaning is found in the following verse:

وَلِلّٰهِ الْاَسْمَآءُ الْحُسْنٰى فَادْعُوهُ بِهَا

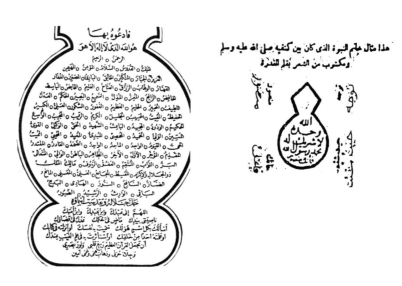

123

****

<u>SURAH II (2)</u> *The Cow*

In the name of Allah, the Beneficent,
the Merciful.

1. Alif. Lam. Mim.

2. This is the Scripture wherein
there is no doubt, a guidance unto
those who ward off (evil):

3. Who believe in the unseen, and
establish worship, and spend of that
We have bestowed upon them;

4. And who believe in that which is
revealed unto thee (Muhammad) and
that which was revealed before thee,
and are certain of the Hereafter.

5. These depend on guidance from
their Lord. These are the successful.

الٓمّٓ ۚ

ذَٰلِكَ ٱلْكِتَٰبُ لَا رَيْبَ ۛ فِيهِ ۛ هُدًى لِّلْمُتَّقِينَ ۚ
ٱلَّذِينَ يُؤْمِنُونَ بِٱلْغَيْبِ وَيُقِيمُونَ ٱلصَّلَوٰةَ وَمِمَّا
رَزَقْنَٰهُمْ يُنفِقُونَ ۚ
وَٱلَّذِينَ يُؤْمِنُونَ بِمَآ أُنزِلَ إِلَيْكَ وَمَآ أُنزِلَ مِن
قَبْلِكَ وَبِٱلْءَاخِرَةِ هُمْ يُوقِنُونَ ۚ
أُو۟لَٰٓئِكَ عَلَىٰ هُدًى مِّن رَّبِّهِمْ ۖ وَأُو۟لَٰٓئِكَ هُمُ
ٱلْمُفْلِحُونَ ۚ

II *Surah Al-Baqqara*, **The Generous Qur'an** 2:1-5

****

124

The Imperative of Knowing Arabic

Some people claim to translate the meaning and conception of the **Generous Qur'an**. But the question that this raises is, which meaning, out of the unfathomable treasure of conceptions that are associated with even one word or one letter or one accent, would a translator choose to write? The **Generous Qur'an** translated into English or French or any other language is not the **Generous Qur'an**. Just by attempting to translate the **Generous Qur'an**, a translator is usually declaring and asserting his pluralistic ignorance. Perhaps translators have good intentions, but they often do not really know what they are facing. In many cases, consciously or unconsciously, they are doing more harm than good to the cause of human understanding of **ALLAH's** (*subhanahu wa ta'ala*) Word. When someone reads a "translation" of the **Generous Qur'an**, it should be known to him or her that this is not the actual word of **ALLAH** (*subhanahu wa ta'ala*), nor is it the **Generous Qur'an** or its meaning. It is, in fact, nor more than the author's limited notion of the meaning of the **Generous Qur'an** that has been sifted through his obstructed vision. Though he might have good intentions, he has asserted and declared his pluralistic ignorance. No human mind can ever duplicate the **Generous Qur'an** nor its conceptions or meaning.

Those who are interested in learning about Islam can have the principles of Islam explained to them, and if they are really committed they may be invited by **ALLAH** (*subhanahu wa ta'ala*) to become Muslims and practice Islam. Then **ALLAH** (*subhanahu wa ta'ala*) will open their hearts and minds to the treasures of His words. They would have to learn Arabic, and experience an

125

ideational metamorphosis in their axiomatic precepts, which will clear and enlighten their cognition and thereby change their fiber and fabric and ultimate frame of reference. At that point they would become true Muslims, reciting and cognitively understanding the **Generous Qur'an** in Arabic, and they would feel the radiating illumination that comes from knowing that **ALLAH** (*subhanahu wa ta'ala*) is addressing them directly when they recite the **Generous Qur'an** in Arabic. Each person in the world must remember that the **Generous Qur'an** in Arabic is the actual Word of **ALLAH** (*subhanahu wa ta'ala*).

There is no more valuable thing in the world than learning the actual language and words of **ALLAH** (*subhanahu wa ta'ala*), Who created this world out of nothingness. Many people in the world seek knowledge and spend years in *kufur* (non-authentic-Islamic) universities such as Harvard, Berkeley, the Sorbonne, or Oxford, etc., getting Ph.D.s in the anticipation of seeking knowledge, only to find out on the day of graduation and commencement that whatever knowledge they learned constitutes the changing values and variables of history. The latter are inapplicable *in toto* to the Order of Things and to the student's present and future. It would be more valuable to learn the Arabic language, which is a must in order to understand the eloquence and profound articulation which rejuvenates yet transcends the human cognition. The Arabic language is the oldest living language that is applicable throughout all stages of history. A person who graduates with a Ph.D. today from the so-called best *kufur* university could not easily understand the books written three hundred years ago even in his own language. He would need to be tutored for anywhere between seven to fifteen years to understand the cognition of one classical

126

Chapter IV. The Generous Qur'an as the Only Authentic Word of ALLAH

author, due to the unfamiliar conceptions, terminology, lexicon, axioms and linguistic differentiations expressed in his writing. Every language except Arabic is encapsulated within the structural, linguistic differentiation between space and time. Arabic is a unique language within itself. By contrast, any person with a simple understanding of Arabic today could easily comprehend any book written in Arabic, even hundreds or thousands of years ago, without any problems or misconceptions.[14] This is because **ALLAH's** (*subhanahu wa ta'ala*) Word governs the world. He made the trajectory of society conform to the lexicon of Arabic and made the Arabic language easy to understand, while simultaneously making it immune from incongruity and misconceptions. Therefore, the Arabic language is a language of the past, present and future. The Arabic language is thus ahistorical, and no other language can come close to it.

Historically, many individuals whom **ALLAH** (*subhanahu wa ta'ala*) led to Islam were not Arabs. However, they learned Arabic and they became the best scholars of Islam and the Arabic language. They wrote volumes and volumes about Islam and the episteme of knowledge in Arabic. Any person who is committed to Islam and knows the real value of being, must learn the Arabic language and fulfill the call of **ALLAH** (*subhanahu wa ta'ala*). With that proper frame of mind, attitude, cognition and heart, the individual will feel that he is coming home to his original state of being, which is as a Muslim. According to Islam, everyone is born a Muslim. Learning Arabic will enrich, purify and crystallize his original state of being, because that person is coming home to his indigenous language. Becoming a Muslim and knowing Arabic will help the individual who has been invited to Islam to

127

metamorphose as he understands the Light, jewels and pearls of the **Generous Qur'an** in the anticipation of learning what it means to be *'Abd* **ALLAH** (the slave of **ALLAH**, *subhanahu wa ta'ala*).

The Particular and Universal Relevance of the Generous Qur'an

Knowing Arabic is an imperative for understanding the **Generous Qur'an**, because **ALLAH** (*subhanahu wa ta'ala*) explicitly said *"Qur'anan Arabiyan"* (an Arabic **Qur'an**). **ALLAH** (*subhanahu wa ta'ala*) governs the Word, the meaning and the consciousness of the reader. Therefore, **ALLAH** (*subhanahu wa ta'ala*) articulates the **Generous Qur'an** in such a way that He makes it applicable to the multiple levels of consciousness of the reader. **ALLAH** (*subhanahu wa ta'ala*) mysteriously amalgamates the Word, the meaning and the reader together in such a profound manner that the meaning is applicable to the time dimension at any particular space and time. That is to say, this amalgamation explains any phenomenon or issue. It deduces its contextual ramification, and articulates and delineates its contextual methodology in an eloquent and profoundly flowing, chronological manner.

It is imperative to understand the chronology of **ALLAH's** (*subhanahu wa ta'ala*) delineation in any verse. Each word constitutes a structural prerequisite for the word that follows, as well as an imperative linkage and structural requisite for understanding the preceding word. All three words together take on infinite saturated conceptual meanings which constitute the inward and outward linkages to understanding any word in its

128

Chapter IV. The Generous Qur'an as the Only Authentic Word of ALLAH

contextually linked meanings. Any one word, two words, or aggregate of three words similarly becomes a conceptual linkage for understanding a broader meaning in conjunction with another verse. This is why the **Generous Qur'an** is an infinite ocean in itself, without a rigid structure. It has its own citadel which is apparent, gigantic and dynamic to the point that the human mind cannot encompass it *in toto*. This is further reason why it also has hidden meanings that only **ALLAH** (*subhanahu wa ta'ala*), and not His slaves, can fathom.[15]

Though the slave of **ALLAH** (*subhanahu wa ta'ala*) cannot fathom the **Generous Qur'an**, it is a blessing from **ALLAH** (*subhanahu wa ta'ala*) that He (*subhanahu wa ta'ala*) lets some of His slaves find refuge in it. Each word or aggregation of words becomes a protective citadel compatible with the particularistic stage of consciousness that humans are passing through. Therefore, regardless of the infinite multiplicity of circumstances in the human condition, one word or verse could be found to describe, delineate and resolve any particular situation. If an individual is pious, **ALLAH** (*subhanahu wa ta'ala*) will mysteriously lead him to the particular word, phrase or sentence that is compatible with and relevant to his particular predicament, time, space and contextual issue. In this manner, one can find refuge and hope. One can know that he is not left alone, but rather **ALLAH** (*subhanahu wa ta'ala*), Who created him, is with him, carrying him over and through all circumstances in his life, whether they are peaceful or they constitute a tribulation.

When *'Abd* **ALLAH** (the servant of **ALLAH**, *subhanahu wa ta'ala*) realizes that the verse he is reading describes his particular circumstances, he is already in the process of metamorphosis from

Chapter IV. The Generous Qur'an as the Only Authentic Word of ALLAH

darkness to light, from despair to confidence, from deviance to straightness, from alienation to oneness, from bitterness to happiness. Therefore, the infinite and unfathomable, universalistic words of **ALLAH** (*subhanahu wa ta'ala*) become particular, confined, precisely delineated, vivid and relevant to the state or station of the particular pious human slave of **ALLAH** (*subhanahu wa ta'ala*). In this manner, the **Generous Qur'an** itself is reading the particular human heart and mind, invading and navigating through the particulars of the human estate.

When the universal **Generous Qur'an** becomes particular, and the particular becomes universal, the slave of **ALLAH** (*subhanahu wa ta'ala*) becomes the inward and outward linkage of the inversion process between the eternal and the temporal, the divine and the mundane, the spiritual and the material, and between what *is* and what is being created.[16] Finally, what is being created is the slave of **ALLAH** (*subhanahu wa ta'ala*), in whom is embedded all the secrets of Creation. Therefore, **ALLAH** (*subhanahu wa ta'ala*) gave and fulfilled His Word, so that His slaves would find guidance to straightness, openness and healthiness as a prelude to their journey back to where they descended from.

One might ask, who is reading the **Generous Qur'an**? The readers of the **Generous Qur'an** in essence came out of nothingness. The biggest mystery of this world is that creation came out of nothingness. It is the Word of **ALLAH** (*subhanahu wa ta'ala*) that made the nothingness into being. Being, in itself, is no more than the manifestation of the Word. As an example, the creation of Adam (*peace be upon him*) was no more than the manifestation of **ALLAH's** (*subhanahu wa ta'ala*) order to "Be!" --and Adam (*peace *be upon him*) was. **ALLAH** (*subhanahu wa ta'ala*) Himself taught Adam (*peace be upon him*) the "names" and order of everything. Therefore, imbedded in every human being are the "names" of the Order of Things. Humans thus have *a priori* knowledge of every particular case.[17] When people learn the Word, they are not really learning something new. When they learn Arabic and they learn a Word from the **Generous Qur'an**, they are, in essence, coming home. They are not learning something alien to themselves, because the Word is the Word of **ALLAH** (*subhanahu wa ta'ala*) and the reader is the creation of **ALLAH** (*subhanahu wa ta'ala*). **ALLAH** (*subhanahu wa ta'ala*) created man to worship Him. Prior to man's creation, **ALLAH** (*subhanahu wa ta'ala*) carved the Word inside him and made the Word an indigenous part of him. Without the Word, man is nothing. Because of that Word in Adam (*peace be upon him),* **ALLAH** (*subhanahu wa ta'ala*) ordered the angels to bow to Adam (*peace be upon him*). When a human becomes conscious of who he truly is, he has to realize that he is the slave of **ALLAH** (*subhanahu wa ta'ala*). This realization will lead him to find the Word in the **Generous Qur'an** that will help him out in any particular situation.

Reading the **Generous Qur'an** is not doing something new. It is a process of reviewing and remembering one's original state. That original state is similar to the process of rebirth. Every newborn is a Muslim by *fitrah* (original essence). Praying, in itself, and reading the **Generous Qur'an**, constitute direct communication between the slave and **ALLAH** (*subhanahu wa ta'ala*). There are many slaves, and therefore there are many particular and different situations. The Word becomes the only linkage between the particular and the universal. Therefore, the Word keeps its hidden and majestic treasure and autonomy on the universal level. This is why the particulars find a word to dwell on in the universal. **ALLAH** (*subhanahu wa ta'ala*) is the Immanent source of both. This is why **ALLAH** (*subhanahu wa ta'ala*) amalgamates the Word, the reader and the meaning together. All this is ultimately nothing except **ALLAH** (*subhanahu wa ta'ala*).

This chapter has involved a discussion of meaning and relevance linking the **Generous Qur'an** with the diversity of human reality. The emphasis was on the **Generous Qur'an** as the only authentic reality. It is important to see, however, that the exclusive authenticity of the **Generous Qur'an** as divine revelation does not imply that the **Generous Qur'an** is only something relevant to the community of Muslim believers. The following chapter, therefore, will delve into the relevance of the **Generous Qur'an** for all humanity.

THE FIRMEST BOND

132

Endnotes

[1] Seyyed Hossein Nasr, *Ideals and Realities of Islam*, (London: George Allen & Unwin, Ltd. 1975). pp. 41-67.

[2] Ibid.

[3] Yaqub Zaki, "The Concept of Revelation in Islam", *Islamic Quarterly*, (Vol. 32), 1988.

[4] Ibid.

[5] Muhammad Al-Ghazzali, *Our Beginning in Wisdom*, (New York: Octagon Books, 1975), pp. 45-50.

[6] Dr. Ahmad Abd Al-Hamid Ghorab, *The Qur'anic Reasoning*, (London: Ta Ha Publishers, Ltd. 1981), pp. 4-18.

[7] Ibid., pp. 25-39.

[8] Mahmoud Shaltout, "Islamic Beliefs and Code of Laws", in *Islam: The Straight Path*, Kenneth W. Morgan, editor. (New York: The Ronald Press Company, 1958), pp. 87-143.

[9] Seyyed Hossein Nasr, *Traditional Islam in the Modern World*, (New York: KPI, 1987), pp. 203-226.

[10] Mahmoud Shaltout, Op. Cit.

11Ibid.

وَمَا تَوْفِيقِي إِلَّا بِاللَّهِ عَلَيْهِ تَوَكَّلْتُ وَإِلَيْهِ أُنِيبُ

12Seyyed Hossein Nasr, *Islamic Life and Thought*, (Albany, New York: State University of New York Press, 1981), pp. 1-7.

13Anwar G. Chejne, *The Arabic Language: Its Role in History*, (Minneapolis, MN: University of Minnesota Press: 1969), pp. 3-24.

14Ibid.

إِنَّ اللَّهَ مَعَنَا

15A. E. Affifi, "The Rational and Mystical Interpretations of Islam", in *Islam: The Straight Path*, Kenneth W. Morgan, editor. (New York: The Ronald Press Company, 1958), pp. 144-179.

16Sir Muhammad Iqbal, *The Reconstruction of Religious Thought in Islam*, (Lahore, Pakistan: Sh. Muhammad Ashraf, 1962), pp. 1-27.

17Seyyed Hossein Nasr, *Ideals and Realities of Islam*, Op. Cit.

134

CHAPTER V

The Generous Qur'an is for All Humanity

****

SURAH II (2) *The Cow*

In the name of Allah, the
Beneficent, the Merciful

1. Alif. Lam. Mim.

2. This is the Scripture wherein
there is no doubt, a guidance unto
those who ward off (evil):

3. Who believe in the unseen, and
establish worship, and spend of that
We have bestowed upon them;

4. And who believe in that which is
revealed unto thee (Muhammad) and
that which was revealed before thee,
and are certain of the Hereafter.

5. These depend on guidance from
their Lord. These are the successful.

سُوْرَةُ الْبَقَرَةِ مَدَنِيَّةٌ وَرُوعَانُهَا

بِسْمِ اللهِ الرَّحْمٰنِ الرَّحِيْمِ ۝

الٓمّٓ ۝

ذٰلِكَ الْكِتٰبُ لَا رَيْبَ فِيْهِ هُدًى لِّلْمُتَّقِيْنَ ۝

الَّذِيْنَ يُؤْمِنُوْنَ بِالْغَيْبِ وَيُقِيْمُوْنَ الصَّلٰوةَ وَمِمَّا رَزَقْنٰهُمْ يُنْفِقُوْنَ ۝

وَالَّذِيْنَ يُؤْمِنُوْنَ بِمَا أُنْزِلَ إِلَيْكَ وَمَا أُنْزِلَ مِنْ قَبْلِكَ وَبِالْاٰخِرَةِ هُمْ يُوْقِنُوْنَ ۝

أُولٰٓئِكَ عَلٰى هُدًى مِّنْ رَّبِّهِمْ وَأُولٰٓئِكَ هُمُ الْمُفْلِحُوْنَ ۝

II *Surah Al-Baqqara*, **The Generous Qur'an** 2:1-5

****

135

Chapter V. The Generous Qur'an is for All Humanity

****

SURAH XXVII (27) *The Ant*

6.   Lo! as for thee (Muhammad), thou verily receivest the Qur'an from the presence of One Wise, Aware.

وَإِنَّكَ لَتُلَقَّى الْقُرْآنَ مِن لَّدُنْ حَكِيمٍ عَلِيمٍ ۝

XXVII *Surah Naml*, **The Generous Qur'an 27:6**

****

SURAH XVII (17) *The Night Journey*

89.   And verily We have displayed for mankind in this Qur'an all kinds of similitudes, but most of mankind refuse aught save disbelief.

وَلَقَدْ صَرَّفْنَا لِلنَّاسِ فِي هَٰذَا الْقُرْآنِ مِن كُلِّ مَثَلٍ فَأَبَىٰ أَكْثَرُ النَّاسِ إِلَّا كُفُورًا ۝

XVII *Surah Israa'*, **The Generous Qur'an 17:89**

****

SURAH XLI (41) *Fussilat*

3.   A Scripture whereof the verses are expounded, a Lecture in Arabic for people Who have knowledge.

كِتَابٌ فُصِّلَتْ آيَاتُهُ قُرْآنًا عَرَبِيًّا لِّقَوْمٍ يَعْلَمُونَ ۝

XLI *Surah Fussilat*, **The Generous Qur'an 41:3**

****

136

****

SURAH XXX (30) *The Romans*

58.   Verily We have coined for mankind in the Qur'an all kinds of similitudes; and indeed if thou camest unto them with a miracle, those who disbelieve would verily exclaim: Ye are but tricksters!

59. Thus doth Allah seal the hearts of those who know not.

60.   So have patience (O Muhammad)! Allah's promise is the very truth, and let not those who have no certainty make thee impatient.

وَلَقَدْ ضَرَبْنَا لِلنَّاسِ فِى هَٰذَا الْقُرْآنِ مِن كُلِّ مَثَلٍ وَلَئِن جِئْتَهُم بِآيَةٍ لَّيَقُولَنَّ الَّذِينَ كَفَرُوٓا۟ إِنْ أَنتُمْ إِلَّا مُبْطِلُونَ ۝

كَذَٰلِكَ يَطْبَعُ اللَّهُ عَلَىٰ قُلُوبِ الَّذِينَ لَا يَعْلَمُونَ ۝

فَاصْبِرْ إِنَّ وَعْدَ اللَّهِ حَقٌّ وَلَا يَسْتَخِفَّنَّكَ الَّذِينَ لَا يُوقِنُونَ ۝

XXX Surah Rum, **The Generous Qur'an** 30:58-60

****

A Prelude to Understanding the Generous Qur'an

It is imperative at this juncture to address the universal relevance of the **Generous Qur'an**. The **Generous Qur'an** was not revealed only for Muslim human beings. It has meaning and relevance with respect to all beings in the creation, including the heavens and the earth, the stars and the trees, the fishes and the

137

Chapter V. The Generous Qur'an is for All Humanity

birds, the Muslims and the non-Muslims.[1] No amount of human writing could completely address all the ways in which this relevance is manifested. Therefore, this chapter will focus on the relation of the **Generous Qur'an** to humanity in particular.

Any human being, regardless of his level of consciousness, and regardless of his belief, could understand the Word of **ALLAH** (*subhanahu wa ta'ala*) in the **Generous Qur'an** to a certain extent. This is because the **Generous Qur'an** is the actual Word of **ALLAH** (*subhanahu wa ta'ala*), and every human being is in actuality the slave of **ALLAH** (*subhanahu wa ta'ala*), (*'Abd* **ALLAH**). The Creator of humankind has created every human being in the anticipation that that human being may understand His Word. An in-depth understanding of the **Generous Qur'an** is contingent upon the light and the consciousness that has been bestowed upon that individual. Each individual has a different level of consciousness that determines the level and the significance of his understanding of the **Generous Qur'an**. The individual's consciousness is thus the key variable determining his understanding of the **Generous Qur'an**.

The **Generous Qur'an** has many infinite levels of meaning whose conception only **ALLAH** (*subhanahu wa ta'ala*) knows. Some individuals could even read the **Generous Qur'an** as literature and understand at least something. Some people who are given to speculation might read the **Generous Qur'an**. They might find something in it and they might not. What any individual understands from the **Generous Qur'an** is contingent, at this level of analysis, upon his level of consciousness. Some people might read it, not in order to believe, but to satisfy their curiosity. This might be a prelude to their involvement in doubt.

With the Will of **ALLAH** (*subhanahu wa ta'ala*), however, through reading the **Generous Qur'an**, people might

138

Chapter V. The Generous Qur'an is for All Humanity

metamorphose from the realm of doubt into the realm of certainty. A person could arrive at the realm of certainty over a day, over a week, over a year, over a decade or over a century, and so on. When an individual arrives at this realm that negates doubt, it means that he is in the process of metamorphosis. The result is that he is on the road of surrendering and becoming a true believer. At that point, the individual is not reading the **Generous Qur'an** as literature, because **ALLAH** (*subhanahu wa ta'ala*) has already opened his heart. He reads and hears, and understands that what he is reading is not casual literature. What he is reading in fact is the most precious, sacred, mysterious and eloquent Word, which in actuality is the only authentic Word of **ALLAH** (*subhanahu wa ta'ala*) that was preserved through the experience of the human melodrama.[2]

If the individual arrives at such a level of consciousness, he is not reading the **Generous Qur'an** with speculation or doubtful perplexity. He is reading some of the mysterious Words of **ALLAH** (*subhanahu wa ta'ala*) through which man himself became a reality. What was in the beginning was negation, in the realm of nothingness, and through the Word of **ALLAH** (*subhanahu wa ta'ala*), existence and the world became reality, and man became what he is. Man can never have a meaning without the world and Word through which he became.

To know what man is, and to understand that he is no more than the slave of **ALLAH** (*subhanahu wa ta'ala*), 'Abd **ALLAH** (*subhanahu wa ta'ala*), a person has to first believe that the **Generous Qur'an** is *pari passu* the Word of **ALLAH** (*subhanahu wa ta'ala*). When he arrives at this level of consciousness, belief in the **Generous Qur'an** will constitute an irrevocable and unequivocal guiding force for him to be what he is, which is no more than *'Abd*

139

ALLAH (*subhanahu wa ta'ala*).[3] At that point there is nothing more valuable for him to do than try to understand in depth and dedicate his life to the Word of **ALLAH** (*subhanahu wa ta'ala*). Such in-depth understanding is an internal journey for man, because man becomes a linkage between negation and existence. Man, reality and the world, in the final analysis, came through the Word of **ALLAH** (*subhanahu wa ta'ala*).

At this juncture, it is necessary to understand that the Word of **ALLAH** (*subhanahu wa ta'ala*) in the **Generous Qur'an** came in the Arabic language.

Translation *vis-á-vis* the Generous Qur'an

No human being could ever fully understand the infinite meaning of the **Generous Qur'an** in Arabic. Therefore, any "translation" of the **Generous Qur'an** is not the Generous Qur'an *per se*. Those who want to translate the **Generous Qur'an** often claim that they are translating its meaning. The question becomes "which meaning?", when each verse of the **Generous Qur'an** has infinite meanings. Each human being is encapsulated within the illusionary interplay between space and time, and so can only convey a limited perspective about any verse.

The issue becomes what a person can do who does not know Arabic, but wants to read the **Generous Qur'an**. A newcomer to Islam, a person newly dedicated to the Word of **ALLAH** (*subhanahu wa ta'ala*), could read a translation of the **Generous Qur'an** in any language while he is learning Arabic. He should understand, however, that the translation is not equivalent to the **Generous Qur'an**. Any such translation contains the words of man *about* the

140

Chapter V. The Generous Qur'an is for All Humanity

Generous Qur'an. The person reading a translation of the **Generous Qur'an** becomes encapsulated within the mind of a human being, who might never encompass the multiplicity of meaning in the **Generous Qur'an**. Reading a translation, therefore, may be beneficial to a certain extent, but not to a significant degree.

If the individual is really committed to **ALLAH** (*subhanahu wa ta'ala*) and nothing occupies him other than the Word of **ALLAH** (*subhanahu wa ta'ala*), he eventually must learn the Arabic language. In learning the Arabic language, in the anticipation of learning the **Generous Qur'an**, that individual is not learning something that is alien to his indigenous human estate. He is learning something that his indigenous human estate was created to do, namely recite the Word of **ALLAH** (*subhanahu wa ta'ala*) in Arabic. If he is really committed to **ALLAH** (*subhanahu wa ta'ala*), he should make surrender to **ALLAH** (*subhanahu wa ta'ala*) and declare vehemently that he is a Muslim. When a person becomes a Muslim he has to pray, because prayer (*salaat*) is one of the main pillars of Islam. When he wants to perform this prayer, he has to perform it in Arabic. It is well-known that **ALLAH** (*subhanahu wa ta'ala*) is glorified in many languages, which include human languages as well as those of the birds and other creatures. **ALLAH** (*subhanahu wa ta'ala*) is being glorified and worshipped in every place and every time. This sometimes occurs through a word, and sometimes through a non-word, that is to say through thinking, crying or bowing, etc.[4]

The crucial issue at this juncture is that **ALLAH** (*subhanahu wa ta'ala*) has said, in a human conceptual meaning, "We are sending down the Word and We are going to preserve it". To preserve His Word, He did not preserve only the Word *per se*, but also the Arabic language. Through understanding the Arabic language, and under the Light bestowed by **ALLAH** (*subhanahu wa*

141

ta'ala), the individual could understand that the meaning present in the original, contextual Word in Arabic is better than in any "translation". When one reads the same verse in Arabic at different times, he will not be encapsulated by a human translation. Human translations of the **Generous Qur'an** are necessarily victims of time, language limitations and the illusion of meanings. Thus, any committed individual who has surrendered and wants to understand with real significance the contextual meaning of the **Generous Qur'an** should dedicate himself to both learning and understanding the Arabic language, as an authentic Arabic speaker, in the anticipation, with the Will of **ALLAH** (*subhanahu wa ta'ala*), of understanding the **Generous Qur'an**.

Dedication to learning Arabic with the goal of understanding the **Generous Qur'an** is an irrevocable and unequivocal indication that the individual has real belief. He does not suffer from a dualistic value system whereby he believes in one thing and practices something else. If he is really a believer, then he will become thrust into reading the **Generous Qur'an** as a guiding force. From this perspective, people who are not Muslims and have no more than a proclamation of knowledge in regard to learning the **Generous Qur'an** and its infinite dimensions of meaning will come to the realization that any conception of reality and the order of things that exists prior to becoming a Muslim and reading the **Generous Qur'an** can be no more than a mirage.

Muslims make a big mistake if they believe that non-Muslim knowledge could ever be used as a tool to conceptualize knowledge itself and its infinite dimensions within the **Generous Qur'an** in any non-Arabic language, or if they try to comprehensively translate the **Generous Qur'an** or its meaning into such a language.[5] The second they do this, they are suffering from an inferiority complex and are being trapped in the realm of mirage. That is to say, the

142

Chapter V. The Generous Qur'an is for All Humanity

concept that has imposed itself on the Muslims under the pretense of the "Islamization of knowledge" is rejected. This concept implies that knowledge exists outside of Islam, in the *kufur* (non-authentic-Islamic) West and East. Some Muslims want to translate such knowledge into Arabic and put an Islamic cliché over it in order to penetrate the Muslim mind. Through this process, the Muslims will be receiving and consuming what the *kufur* West and East have speculated and theorized. Thereby, the *kufar* (infidels) will have temporarily succeeded in calling Muslims to their deviant *kufur* ways, under the pretense of *kufur* rational deliberation and "scientificity". This is simply another approach to de-Islamizing the Muslims, because it encourages Muslims to glorify something that is not Islamic.

The authentic Islamic approach represents the total opposite. This approach implies belief in the **Generous Qur'an** as a guiding force that has embedded within it the totality of knowledge. It also indicates that if any one, regardless of his race, color or language affiliation, wants to understand the **Generous Qur'an**, it is imperative for him to learn the Arabic language. Through this approach, the Muslims and the Arabs in general are conveying the treasures they have to the rest of the world. They are helping those in the *kufur* West and the *kufur* East, who are victims of illusionary, speculative knowledge, to metamorphose ideationally and cognitively in their fiber and fabric in order to surrender and submit to **ALLAH** (*subhanahu wa ta'ala*), and become Muslims. This is the real concept of *da'wah*, (calling people through knowledge to **ALLAH** (*subhanahu wa ta'ala*) and to Islam).[6]

When this call is truly manifested, an individual, regardless of his spatial location, may come to grips with the reality that the **Generous Qur'an** is the only authentic Word of **ALLAH** (*subhanahu wa ta'ala*). Through time, he will come to embody this

143

belief. When he believes that the **Generous Qur'an** is the authentic Word of **ALLAH** (*subhanahu wa ta'ala*), he starts to understand the **Generous Qur'an** as a guiding force. This sometimes occurs instantaneously, sometimes over time.

One has to remember that many of the great writers of Islam originally were not native speakers of Arabic. However, when they came to grips with the fact that the **Generous Qur'an** is the only authentic Word of **ALLAH** (*subhanahu wa ta'ala*), they learned the Arabic language, regardless of their age, location or interest. Learning the Arabic language was of a great value in the development of a vivid vision of the meticulous, profound and eloquent way of understanding reality. That understanding will help every individual to metamorphose into what he really is, which is no more than a slave of **ALLAH** (*subhanahu wa ta'ala*). When the individual becomes conscious that he is the slave of **ALLAH** (*subhanahu wa ta'ala*), and has an irrevocable and unequivocal belief in **ALLAH** (*subhanahu wa ta'ala*), as well as in the **Generous Qur'an** as a guiding force, then he is what he really is. His being is no other than that of a slave of **ALLAH** (*subhanahu wa ta'ala*). This is the process through which he could open his heart, his vision, his hearing and his seeing. As a result, he will be in a process of self-annihilation in order to overcome, to really hear, see and be. This being has no realm of "I am", only dwelling in and taking refuge in **ALLAH's** (*subhanahu wa ta'ala*) Word. This is the highest form of being.[7] At that point, the individual is on a journey to understand the Word of **ALLAH** (*subhanahu wa ta'ala*), which in itself is infinite. That Word is imbedded in him, because he is the perfection and the result of that Word. In reality there is nothing except His Word.

Belief in the Generous Qur'an as a Guiding Force

As discussed above, in order to understand the **Generous Qur'an**, it is imperative to understand the Arabic language because the **Generous Qur'an** in any other language is not the **Generous Qur'an**. No other language is capable of articulating profoundly and eloquently the multiplicity of meanings of the **Generous Qur'anic** verses in Arabic. This is due to the structural and grammatical limitations of other languages. The **Generous Qur'an**, in Arabic, is a Book without any crookedness or mistakes because it is bestowed upon humanity from **ALLAH** (*subhanahu wa ta'ala*), Who is the All-Knowing and the All-Wise. It is *ahuman*, meaning to say that it is not made by humans. This is why it is not encapsulated within human limitations or the illusionary interplay between space and time. Therefore, the **Generous Qur'an** encompasses a delineation of every issue in the world and gives us an example *par excellence* as to how each issue should be raised, its methodological apparatus, its conceptual and contextual framework, its *modus operandi* and *modus vivendi*, as well as its empirical ramifications in terms of a solution based upon an authentic, irrevocable and absolute frame of reference.[8]

ALLAH (*subhanahu wa ta'ala*) revealed unto the **Prophet Muhammad** (*prayers and peace of ALLAH be upon him*) "The Book", *pari passu*, the **Generous Qur'an**, as an exposition which articulates and delineates the order of everything. It is a guidance and blessing which forecasts good news for the Muslims.

It is imperative to understand that there are two interrelated issues that need to be comprehended at this level of the exposé. First of all, the **Generous Qur'an** is in the Arabic language, in which its imutable and inimitable verses are delineated and explained in

145

Chapter V. The Generous Qur'an is for All Humanity

detail and to the final touch for those people who have authentic knowledge. Furthermore, within the **Generous Qur'an**, **ALLAH** (*subhanahu wa ta'ala*) propounded every kind of allegorical parable and example *par excellence* so that humans could understand how to live straight and normal lives. Though the **Generous Qur'an** is in Arabic, contains allegorical parables in it for all humankind and is directed to all the world, there are still some people, *qua* humanoids, whose hearts are sick and rusted because they rejected faith. **ALLAH** (*subhanahu wa ta'ala*) does not want to cleanse their hearts. Some of them reside in the zone of indifference regarding the **Generous Qur'an**.[9]

* *

SURAH II (2) *The Cow*

10. In their hearts is a disease, and Allah increaseth their disease. A painful doom is theirs because they lie.

فِى قُلُوبِهِم مَّرَضٌ فَزَادَهُمُ اللَّهُ مَرَضاً وَلَهُمْ عَذَابٌ أَلِيمٌ بِمَا كَانُوا يَكْذِبُونَ ۝

II *Surah Al-Baqqara,* **The Generous Qur'an** 2:10

* *

As mentioned above some humans might read the **Generous Qur'an** as a piece of literature. They might respect it for its profound articulation but go no further than that. Other humans reject the **Generous Qur'an** completely as a frame of reference and become infidels (*kufar*). Other people might accept some parts of it and not other parts. These are the hypocrites and their status will be in the lowest part of the lowest station in Hell. Other people may

146

read the **Generous Qur'an** and understand nothing. These are the people whose hearts are stained and rusted. Then, there are some people who hear it but don't listen to its message because they are engulfed by and obsessed with the call of *Shaytan* (Satan). There are many other types of people that only **ALLAH** (*subhanahu wa ta'ala*) can categorize, such as those who are arrogant and who say they hear but then disobey. Then there are those who say "we hear and we obey". These are the ones whom **ALLAH** (*subhanahu wa ta'ala*) blessed and guided. There are also many other types that a person cannot know of.

Knowing Arabic Alone is Not Enough

It is imperative to understand that reading the **Generous Qur'an** as a guiding force is different from reading it as literature, or for any other reason. This exposé has already emphasized that in order to understand the **Generous Qur'an** as a guiding force it is imperative that one must read it in Arabic. If a person is a true believer and cannot read it in Arabic, he could try to read it in translation, though he has to realize that then he is not reading the **Generous Qur'an** *per se*. **ALLAH** (*subhanahu wa ta'ala*) might give the true believer who does not understand Arabic some light, but if that true believer wants to understand the **Generous Qur'an** to a significant degree of contextual meaning, he has to learn Arabic, in the anticipation of reading and understanding the mystery of **ALLAH's** (*subhanahu wa ta'ala*) Word.[10] Knowing Arabic is imperative, but knowing Arabic alone, without believing in the

147

Chapter V. The Generous Qur'an is for All Humanity

Generous Qur'an as the authentic Word of **ALLAH** (*subhanahu wa ta'ala*), is not enough.

Many Arabs in the time of our **Prophet Muhammad** (*prayers and peace of* **ALLAH** *be upon him*) knew Arabic very well. Some of these Arabs, prior to becoming Muslims, were stunned by the meticulous, profound and simplistic articulation of the **Generous Qur'an**. Some of the main experts and leaders in the Arabic language at that time, who made profound Arabic articulation their vocation, explicitly indicated that this **Generous Qur'an** is so beautiful, so eloquent, so sophisticated, so mysterious and so majestic that it could not be the word of a human being. Some of these giants of the Arabic language at the time of the **Qur'anic** revelation came to a dead-end when they heard it and yet could not believe in it. Those who heard it and believed that it is the Word of the Majestic **ALLAH** (*subhanahu wa ta'ala*) were under pressure from their Arab protegés, who did not believe in it, to think that it represented a force of magic.[11]

Simply put, some people, who had been infidels before hearing the **Generous Qur'an**, turned around 180 degrees from being totally against Islam to becoming the main defenders of Islam. This was the case with 'Umar Ibn Al-Khattab. When he was vehemently against the Muslims, he went with great anger to see his sister, whom he had just been told was a Muslim. At the door, he heard her reciting this Book, the **Generous Qur'an**. The net result was that 'Umar, one of those most inimical to Islam, became a Muslim, and in fact became one of the bravest giants in protecting Islam. For example, when the **Prophet Muhammad** (*prayers and peace of* **ALLAH** *be upon him*) and many of his companions made *hijra* (the emigration to the Arabian city of *Madinah Al-*

148

Chapter V. The Generous Qur'an is for All Humanity

Munawwarah (Medina) from *Makkah Al-Mukarramah* (Mecca)) in secret, 'Umar Ibn Al-Khattab refused to make it in secret. He declared that anyone wishing to make his own wife a widow and/or to make his own children to be orphans should meet him in the valley. He later became the second Caliph of the Muslim community.

It is imperative to understand that knowing Arabic by itself is not enough. The heart of the reader must surrender to **ALLAH** (*subhanahu wa ta'ala*) and he must declare himself to be a Muslim. After declaring that he is a Muslim, he should live according to the *Shari'ah* (the Divine Law of **ALLAH**,*subhanahu wa ta'ala*). When a person becomes a Muslim, and lives according to the Law of **ALLAH** (*subhanahu wa ta'ala*), his heart will be cleansed. This is significant because the mind is located in the heart. At that point, he will see that this **Generous Qur'an** is beyond human consciousness, and he will appreciate it. The more he reads it and the more he practices Islam, and becomes the embodiment of the **Generous Qur'an**, the more the **Generous Qur'an** will reveal itself to him. As a result, the **Generous Qur'an** becomes a guiding force for that individual. If the individual is a pillar in Arabic poetry, literature, grammar, or sociology, etc., but is not a Muslim and a true believer, he will not receive a guiding force through the **Generous Qur'an**. Nevertheless, he will find that the **Generous Qur'an** does not represent a human way, and is not a product of human deliberation. If **ALLAH** (*subhanahu wa ta'ala*) wants to guide him, and remove his heart from the realm of being a non-Muslim to the realm of Islam, **ALLAH** (*subhanahu wa ta'ala*) will mysteriously crystallize His power for that individual. Simultaneously, the individual has to listen to his inner voice.

149

Chapter V. The Generous Qur'an is for All Humanity

When he becomes a Muslim, he should not be involved in hypocrisy, because this tendency causes the heart to be filled with rust, the result being that the individual becomes deaf, dumb and blind. In short, a person might understand nothing from the Arabic word of the **Generous Qur'an**, even though he may be a main pillar of the Arabic language and its poetry.[12]

At the time that **ALLAH** (*subhanahu wa ta'ala*) caused the **Generous Qur'an** to descend, the Arabs were at the peak of skill in poetry. They were very proud of the profound eloquence of their articulation. One piece of poetry might be the cause of a war between one tribe and another. One piece of poetry might produce peace between one tribe and another. Poetry in the Arabic language has a certain structural formation, which is called "balance". Each balance is said to be like an ocean. Each ocean has a phonetic measurement and has to be put profoundly and eloquently, to the final touch, to fit the modelling system of that balance. In Arabic, this is called *"buhoor al-sha'r"*, or the oceans of poetry. Each poem must have a rhythm. To be able to produce these poems with a political, social, psychological or religious, etc., meaning, a person has to be extremely sophisticated in the conception of things, as well as in the grammar, literature and history of the Arabic language.[13] A poet in this situation cannot make a mistake, or he will declare his ignorance.

The **Generous Qur'an** has challenged the pillars of this poetic tradition in general, and the infidel "hawks", "doves" and "eagles" of the *Quraysh* tribe (the dominant tribe in Mecca at the time of the descent of the **Generous Qur'an**) in particular, to produce something like the **Generous Qur'an**. At one point, the challenge was to bring something similar to the **Generous Qur'an** *in toto.*

150

Chapter V. The Generous Qur'an is for All Humanity

Another challenge was to produce one chapter like those of the **Generous Qur'an**. Finally, the challenge was to produce even one verse. Those challenged were asked to produce a likeness either in profound articulation or in conception. The Arab scholars stood stunned, crippled and paralyzed. They were unable to produce even one verse similar to those of the **Generous Qur'an**. Various tribes paid some of these scholars money and gave them a span of time in which to try to take up this challenge. The result was that these scholars, after deep deliberation, declared that they could not produce anything like the **Generous Qur'an**, because the latter is ahuman. They became depressed, and declared their apathy and bankruptcy. This is because no force in the world could ever produce something like what **ALLAH** (*subhanahu wa ta'ala*) produces.

Knowing the Arabic language alone is not enough to make one believe in and see the **Generous Qur'an** as a guiding Way. There are many scholars of the Arabic language, whether they are Arabs or not, who can write beautiful Arabic poetry and understand the mechanisms of the Arabic language in depth as well as the structural formation of its prose and clauses. Nevertheless, they might focus on the **Generous Qur'an** only as a beautiful piece of literature, not as anything more than that. Those individuals whose vision is obstructed and truncated might have a superficial and cosmetic understanding, but they do not see the **Generous Qur'an** as a guide for their *modus operandi* and *modus vivendi*. Knowing Arabic alone, therefore, is not the main issue in understanding the **Generous Qur'an** as a guiding force in life. Nevertheless, it plays a major role in rectifying an individual to Islam. The **Generous Qur'an** came in the language of the Arab

151

people of the *Quraysh* tribe at a time when they had arrived at the apogee and heyday of profound articulation and expression in the Arabic language in terms of poetry and prose. Some of the Arabs who were very articulate in the Arabic language, at the time of the **Qur'anic** revelation were stunned by the **Generous Qur'an**, and became Muslims. Other Arabs from the *Quraysh* tribe, who were of the same high calibre of prestige and articulation in Arabic at that time, rejected the **Generous Qur'an** as a revelation, even though they admired and respected it due to its inimitability and majesty.[14]

Knowing Arabic is not enough for understanding the **Generous Qur'an** as a guiding force. For the individual to be able to understand the **Generous Qur'an** as a guiding force, he must fulfill and be the embodiment of the structural requisites that **ALLAH** (*subhanahu wa ta'ala*) delineated in the **Generous Qur'an**. **ALLAH** (*subhanahu wa ta'ala*) made six complete requisites which are intermingled and cannot be dissected one from the other. Those individuals who have *taqwa* (piety) become the embodiment of these requisites. Each of the requisites are displayed in differing degrees in individuals as a result of **ALLAH's** (*subhanahu wa ta'ala*) kindness and generosity with people. Nevertheless, as a preliminary step towards understanding the **Generous Qur'an** as a significant guiding force in its contextual manifestation, one must become a Muslim.

This does not mean that a person who is not a Muslim cannot understand the **Generous Qur'an**, with certain limitations. The Arabs, in the time of the **Prophet Muhammad** (*prayers and peace of* **ALLAH** *be upon him*) were *kufar* (non-Muslims). Some of them, however, understood some dimensions of the Word, and asserted that it was not a human Word. Some believed in it, and

152

Chapter V. The Generous Qur'an is for All Humanity

others did not. For those who believed in it, a simple understanding of the Word constituted a step toward making surrender and embracing Islam. Paradoxically, by the same token, the **Generous Qur'an** is for every person, whether Arab or non-Arab, Muslim or non-Muslim. Anyone could understand a certain limited meaning from it. A true Muslim, on the other hand, to a certain extent, will understand it as a guiding force, contingent upon his level of belief. This contingency might lead some of the "People of the Book", (those who have received a partial revelation and a portion of the Scripture), including Christian and priests and monks, to understand the **Generous Qur'an** to a certain extent. This is because **ALLAH** (*subhanahu wa ta'ala*) revealed some dimension of truth to them. When they read the **Generous Qur'an**, it makes an echo in their hearts, and their eyes begin to flood with tears. These tears are not fabricated tears, but are a reflection of how **ALLAH** (*subhanahu wa ta'ala*) has crystallized His Power to them, and invaded and navigated through their chests and hearts. Their hearts do not belong to them, but to **ALLAH** (*subhanahu wa ta'ala*), and are between the fingers of the Most Merciful and Compassionate, Who can move them any way He wishes.

153

* *

SURAH V (5) *The Table Spread*

82. Thou wilt find the most vehement of mankind in hostility to those who believe (to be) the Jews, and the idolaters. And thou wilt find the nearest of them in affection to those who believe (to be) those who say: Lo! We are Christians. That is because there are among them priests and monks, and because they are not proud.

83. When they listen to that which hath been revealed unto the messenger, thou seest their eyes overflow with tears because of their recognition of the Truth. They say: Our Lord, we believe. Inscribe us as among the witnesses.

لَتَجِدَنَّ أَشَدَّ النَّاسِ عَدَاوَةً لِّلَّذِينَ آمَنُوا الْيَهُودَ
وَالَّذِينَ أَشْرَكُوا وَلَتَجِدَنَّ أَقْرَبَهُم مَّوَدَّةً لِّلَّذِينَ
آمَنُوا الَّذِينَ قَالُوا إِنَّا نَصَارَى ذَلِكَ بِأَنَّ مِنْهُمْ
قِسِّيسِينَ وَرُهْبَانًا وَأَنَّهُمْ لَا يَسْتَكْبِرُونَ ۝
وَإِذَا سَمِعُوا مَا أُنزِلَ إِلَى الرَّسُولِ تَرَى أَعْيُنَهُمْ
تَفِيضُ مِنَ الدَّمْعِ مِمَّا عَرَفُوا مِنَ الْحَقِّ يَقُولُونَ
رَبَّنَا آمَنَّا فَاكْتُبْنَا مَعَ الشَّاهِدِينَ ۝

V *Surah Al-Ma'ida*, **The Generous Qur'an** 5:82-83

* *

ALLAH (*subhanahu wa ta'ala*) crystallizes His power to whoever He wants. This power becomes a process of ideational metamorphosis within the cognitions and selves of individuals, the result of which is that they are in the process of becoming Muslims. They cannot become true believers unless they make submission to

154

ALLAH (*subhanahu wa ta'ala*), and vehemently declare the *shahada* (the bearing of witness) that there is no god except **ALLAH** (*subhanahu wa ta'ala*), and that **Muhammad** (*prayers and peace of* **ALLAH** *be upon him*) is His Messenger. It is thus imperative to understand that every human being, regardless of his or her tribal affiliation, race or other frame of reference, could understand the Word to a certain degree. The question becomes how a person could *not* understand the Word while he himself is a manifestation of the Word. **ALLAH** (*subhanahu wa ta'ala*) has articulated in the **Generous Qur'an** a phrase that could be interpreted in English as "and in your own essences, don't you see?"

People must keep in mind that Adam (*peace be upon him*) was in the realm of nothingness, and he came into being through the Word. Similarly, when Jesus (*peace be upon him*) was in the realm of nothingness, he came into being through the Word. Every human being was in the realm of nothingness, and through the Word of **ALLAH** (*subhanahu wa ta'ala*), that human being became a reality. Prior to creating him or her, **ALLAH** (*subhanahu wa ta'ala*) prepared that person to understand and remember His Word.[15]

Islam as a Medium of Metamorphosis

The first step to understanding the **Generous Qur'an** as a guiding force is in surrendering to **ALLAH** (*subhanahu wa ta'ala*) and declaring that one is a Muslim. The process of transformation from being a Muslim to becoming a true believer is through understanding the *praxis* of Islam and becoming the embodiment of

155

the Word of **ALLAH** (*subhanahu wa ta'ala*) as manifested in the **Generous Qur'an.** The infinite teaching and meaning of the Word are an eternal metamorphosis for the individual. This infinite meaning made those who are dedicated to His Word to totally surrender.

The first step to understanding the **Generous Qur'an** as a real guiding force is for one to become a Muslim, and surrender and submit to the call of **ALLAH** (*subhanahu wa ta'ala*). When one becomes a Muslim in his or her *modus operandi* and *modus vivendi*, then the **Generous Qur'an** becomes a guiding force. Some of the Arabs at the time of the **Prophet Muhammad**(*prayers and peace of* **ALLAH** *be upon him*) came and told him that "we are true believers" (in Arabic, *"amanna"*), because they had declared the *shahada*. **ALLAH** (*subhanahu wa ta'ala*) answered them immediately by telling them not to say they believed but first to say *"aslamna"*, meaning that they had entered Islam and submitted to **ALLAH** (*subhanahu wa ta'ala*). Then when faith and belief entered their hearts, and when they obeyed **ALLAH** (*subhanahu wa ta'ala*) and the **Prophet Muhammad** (*prayers and peace of* **ALLAH** *be upon him*), they could consider themselves believers. This is because true believers are those who believe in **ALLAH** (*subhanahu wa ta'ala*) and His **Prophet** (*prayers and peace of* **ALLAH** *be upon him*) and they never dispute or doubt that faith. Furthermore, they make *Jihad* (holy struggle) with their wealth and personal belongings in the cause of **ALLAH** (*subhanahu wa ta'ala*). Also, they should not feel that they had done the **Prophet** (*prayers and peace of* **ALLAH** *be upon him*) a favor by becoming Muslims, for indeed **ALLAH** (*subhanahu wa ta'ala*) had done them a favor by leading them to Islam.

156

* *

SURAH XLIX (49) *The Private
Apartments*

14. The wandering Arabs say: We believe. Say (unto them, O Muhammad): Ye believe not, but rather say "We submit," for the faith hath not yet entered into your hearts. Yet, if ye obey Allah and His messenger, He will not withhold from you aught of (the reward of) your deeds. Lo! Allah is Forgiving, Merciful.

15. The (true) believers are those only who believe in Allah and His messenger and afterward doubt not, but strive with their wealth and their lives for the cause of Allah. Such are the sincere.

قَالَتِ الْأَعْرَابُ آمَنَّا قُل لَّمْ تُؤْمِنُوا وَلَكِن قُولُوٓا
اَسْلَمْنَا وَلَمَّا يَدْخُلِ الْإِيمَانُ فِي قُلُوبِكُمْ وَإِن
تُطِيعُوا اللَّهَ وَرَسُولَهُ لَا يَلِتْكُم مِّنْ أَعْمَالِكُمْ شَيْئًا
إِنَّ اللَّهَ غَفُورٌ رَّحِيمٌ ۝
إِنَّمَا الْمُؤْمِنُونَ الَّذِينَ آمَنُوا بِاللَّهِ وَرَسُولِهِ ثُمَّ
لَمْ يَرْتَابُوا وَجَاهَدُوا بِأَمْوَالِهِمْ وَأَنفُسِهِمْ فِي
سَبِيلِ اللَّهِ أُولَٰئِكَ هُمُ الصَّادِقُونَ ۝

XLIX *Surah Hujarat*, **The Generous Qur'an** 49:14-15

* *

First of all, **ALLAH** (*subhanahu wa ta'ala*) has to ordain it and invite His slave to the Straight Path. Then the slave has to respond to the call, declare the *shahada* (witnessing that there is no

157

The Arabic, Qur'anic and Islamic Paradigm:
Light, Jewels and Pearls

Chapter V. The Generous Qur'an is for All Humanity

god except **ALLAH**, *subhanahu wa ta'ala*, and that **Muhammad,** *prayers and peace of* **ALLAH** *be upon him*, is His Messenger). This indicates that he is a Muslim. Then the slave must rectify his life, his *modus operandi* and *modus vivendi* according to the Law of **ALLAH** (*subhanahu wa ta'ala*). This constitutes the first step towards being a true Muslim. After a period of time, through making a commitment to the *praxis* of Islam, the individual will metamorphose from one level of consciousness to a higher one, a level of belief. Thereby he will become a believer.[16] The individual transforms from having a mere historical or cultural association with Islam to being a firm adherent committed to Islam, as a prelude to becoming a believer. Believing is one of the six inseparable requisites for having *taqwa* (piety). Having *taqwa* is the foremost criterion which a person must embody as a prelude to understanding the **Generous Qur'an** as a guiding force. Embodying *taqwa* is the irrevocable and unequivocal requisite for anyone to understand the **Generous Qur'an** (regardless of that person's race, tribe, gender, nationality or linguistic affiliation) in the Eyes of **ALLAH** (*subhanahu wa ta'ala*), Who created mankind from one self. That self is manifested in male and female genders, and different tribes, groupings and nations. **ALLAH** (*subhanahu wa ta'ala*) affirms in the above *Surah Hujarat, Ayah* 13, that out of all His people, the best and most honored of them are those who have *taqwa*. Having *taqwa* is not based on the criterion of knowing one language or another, or of being from one tribe or another. It is based on six inseparable requisites, the first of which is belief in the Unseen. A person cannot have *taqwa* without being a believer. Next, a person cannot be a believer without being a Muslim.

158

Chapter V. The Generous Qur'an is for All Humanity

ALLAH (*subhanahu wa ta'ala*) explains the rest of these requirements as follows:

****

SURAH II (2) *The Cow*

In the name of Allah, the
Beneficent, the Merciful

1. Alif. Lam. Mim.

2.   This is the Scripture wherein there is no doubt, a guidance unto those who ward off (evil):

3. Who believe in the unseen, and establish worship, and spend of that We have bestowed upon them;

4. And who believe in that which is revealed unto thee (Muhammad) and that which was revealed before thee, and are certain of the Hereafter.

5. These depend on guidance from their Lord. These are the successful.

اَلَمَّ ﴿١﴾ سُوْرَةُ الْبَقَرَةِ مَدَنِيَّةٌ رُبُعَانِهَا

بِسْمِ اللهِ الرَّحْمٰنِ الرَّحِيْمِ ۟

الٓمّ ۚ ۟

ذٰلِكَ الْكِتٰبُ لَا رَيْبَ ۛ فِيْهِ ۛ هُدًى لِّلْمُتَّقِيْنَ ۟

الَّذِيْنَ يُؤْمِنُوْنَ بِالْغَيْبِ وَيُقِيْمُوْنَ الصَّلٰوةَ وَمِمَّا رَزَقْنٰهُمْ يُنْفِقُوْنَ ۟

وَالَّذِيْنَ يُؤْمِنُوْنَ بِمَا اُنْزِلَ اِلَيْكَ وَمَا اُنْزِلَ مِنْ قَبْلِكَ وَبِالْاٰخِرَةِ هُمْ يُوْقِنُوْنَ ۟

اُولٰٓئِكَ عَلٰى هُدًى مِّنْ رَّبِّهِمْ وَاُولٰٓئِكَ هُمُ الْمُفْلِحُوْنَ ۟

II *Surah Al-Baqqara*, **The Generous Qur'an 2:1-5**

****

159

Even though these six requisites are all interrelated, we will only discuss in detail two of them: the belief in the Unseen and the establishment of regular prayer.

The Negation of Doubt

It is imperative to understand that the **Generous Qur'an** is the Book without any doubt that gives guidance in its contextual parts and in its totality. This guidance is not for all humankind, not for all the "intellectuals", not for all the orientalists, and not for all the professionals, etc. The **Generous Qur'an** is guidance only to those who have *taqwa*, regardless of their degree of intellectual orientation, professional apparatus or wealth. In order for a human to be able to see in the **Generous Qur'an** a guiding force, he has to have *taqwa*. Regardless of the individual's intellectual status, how well-read he is, how many degrees he has or how many books he has published, if he is not a Muslim believer and does not have *taqwa*, his heart is rusted and his truncated vision is in reality blindness. From the Islamic perspective, he is in the dark. He is at war with himself and with **ALLAH** (*subhanahu wa ta'ala*). He will never see the **Generous Qur'an** as a book of guidance because he has not been invited to the Straight Path.[17] He has instead been engulfed by *Shaytan*, and in many cases he *is Shaytan*. All the universities in the world which do not adhere to Islam, surrender to **ALLAH** (*subhanahu wa ta'ala*) and teach and integrate the **Generous Qur'an** in every discipline of the so-called sciences are only declaring their pluralistic ignorance, without exception, because only the **Generous Qur'an** is the real proof of the Truth.

160

Chapter V. The Generous Qur'an is for All Humanity

Those who read the **Generous Qur'an** without making
submission to **ALLAH** (*subhanahu wa ta'ala*) or performing the
salaat (Islamic prayers) are unclean and cannot touch the **Generous
Qur'an**. How can they see guidance in it when *Shaytan* has made
them to be obsessed with other things? These people are *Shaytan's*
prototypes, trying to fill the minds of his prospective humanoids
with speculations and theories carved with uncertainties. This is
why the above verses include the words "without any doubt".
Whether people believe in existentialism, Marxism, structuralism,
secular humanism, neutral civility, or whatever way other than
Islam, they are engulfed by doubt as to their basis of legitimacy. The
spectrum of their vision and cognition is colored with doubt. By
their own admission, they claim that they cannot understand reality
in toto; they can only develop a conceptual framework based on
doubt. They consider their conceptual frameworks as substitutes for
reality because they cannot deal with reality. They are right, because
a doubtful mind is not prepared to perceive reality. In order to
perceive reality one has to be cleansed of doubt, and exist in the
realm of certainty.

It is apparent that Islam tries to cleanse humankind of
obsession with doubt, which is crooked perception that can never
lead to the Straight Path. Before a person can read the **Generous
Qur'an** and find within it guidance, he has to be straight in his
modus operandi, in his *modus vivendi* and in his belief. There is
no straightness outside Islam. Every other way is crooked. This is
why the opening *Surah* of the **Generous Qur'an** says "guide us to
the *straight* path", (*Surah Fatiha: Ayah* 6). The straightness of
ALLAH's (*subhanahu wa ta'ala*) Way makes the Muslims straight
who adhere to that way. Once one is on the Straight Way, the
modus operandi and *modus vivendi* of the Way itself will prepare

161

Chapter V. The Generous Qur'an is for All Humanity

the individual to gain *taqwa* as a prelude to perceiving guidance in the contextual totality of the **Generous Qur'an**. *Taqwa* negates doubt and uncertainty, and affirms certainty, which is the manifestation of straightness.[18]

Having discussed various religious, historical and linguistic dimensions of understanding the **Generous Qur'an**, the exposé will now address, in the following chapter, details of the Islamic paradigm for belief. Since belief is essential, from the Islamic perspective, for an understanding of the **Generous Qur'an** as a guiding force, it is necessary to examine the prerequisites and the approach to Islamic belief, as a prelude to attaining to such an understanding.

162

Endnotes

[1]William Chittick, "The Words of the All-Merciful", *Parabola*, (vol. VIII, no. 3), pp. 18-25.

[2]Seyyed Hossein Nasr, *Islamic Life and Thought*, (Albany, NY: State University of New York Press, 1981), pp. 191-199.

[3]Taqee Ad-Deen Ibn Taymiyah, *Al-'Uboodiyah: The Essay of Worship*, (Elizabeth, New Jersey: Daar Al-Hadeeth, 1987), pp. 23-54.

[4]Ibid., pp. 72-91.

[5]Muhammad Abul Quasem (translator), *The Jewels of the Qur'an: Al-Ghazali's Theory*, (London: Kegan Paul International, 1977, 1983), pp. 12-27.

[6]Charles Le Gai Eaton, *Islam and the Destiny of Man*, (Albany, New York: State University of New York Press/Islamic Texts Society, 1985), pp. 9-19.

[7]Faqir Nur Muhammad Sarwari Qadri, *Irfan: A True and Unique Book of Divine Knowledge*, (Lahore, Pakistan: Ripon Printing Press. n.d.), pp. 92-126.

[8]Charles Wendell (translator), *Five Tracts of Hasan Al-Banna'*, (Berkeley, California: University of California Press, 1978), pp. 70-99.

[9]Ibid.

[10]A. L. Tibawi, *Arabic and Islamic Themes: Historical, Educational and Literary Studies,* (London: Luzac & Company, 1974), pp. 72-98.

[11]Ibid., pp. 86-98.

[12]Ibid.

[13]Fazlur Rahman, *Islam,* (New York: Holt, Rinehart and Winston, 1966), pp. 30-42.

[14]Philip K. Hitti, *History of the Arabs: From the Earliest Times to the Present,* (London: Macmillan and Co., 1970), pp. 617-694.

[15]Seyyed Hossein Nasr, Op. Cit.

[16]Sheikh Muzaffer Ozak Al-Jerrahi, *The Unveiling of Love: Sufism and the Remembrance of God,* (New York: Inner Traditions International, 1981), pp.99-115.

[17]Arberry, A.J. (translator), *The Discourses of Rumi,* (New York: Samuel Weiser, 1972), pp. 113-189.

[18]Charles Wendell, Op. Cit., pp. 42-67.

Chapter VI

An Islamic Paradigm for Belief

****

SURAH II (2) *The Cow*

In the name of Allah, the
Beneficent, the Merciful

1. Alif. Lam. Mim.

2. This is the Scripture wherein
there is no doubt, a guidance unto
those who ward off (evil):

3. Who believe in the unseen, and
establish worship, and spend of that
We have bestowed upon them;

4. And who believe in that which
is revealed unto thee (Muhammad)
and that which was revealed before
thee, and are certain of the Hereafter.

5. These depend on guidance from
their Lord. These are the successful.

أَيَاتُهَا (٢) سُورَةُ الْبَقَرَةِ مَدَنِيَّةٌ وُكُوعَاتُهَا

بِسْمِ اللهِ الرَّحْمٰنِ الرَّحِيْمِ ۝

الٓمٓ ۝

ذٰلِكَ الْكِتٰبُ لَارَيْبَ فِيْهِ هُدًى لِّلْمُتَّقِيْنَ ۝

الَّذِيْنَ يُؤْمِنُوْنَ بِالْغَيْبِ وَيُقِيْمُوْنَ الصَّلٰوةَ وَمِمَّا رَزَقْنٰهُمْ يُنْفِقُوْنَ ۝

وَالَّذِيْنَ يُؤْمِنُوْنَ بِمَا أُنْزِلَ إِلَيْكَ وَمَا أُنْزِلَ مِنْ قَبْلِكَ وَبِالْاٰخِرَةِ هُمْ يُوْقِنُوْنَ ۝

أُولٰٓئِكَ عَلٰى هُدًى مِّنْ رَّبِّهِمْ وَأُولٰٓئِكَ هُمُ الْمُفْلِحُوْنَ ۝

II *Surah Al-Baqqara*, **The Generous Qur'an 2:1-5**

****

165

Belief in the Unseen vs. the Seen

It is imperative that any reader who is seeking to understand the **Generous Qur'an** start with the **Generous Qur'an** itself. All of the **Generous Qur'an** is guidance for those who have piety. For any human being who is metamorphosed and ideationally transferred to a state of piety, the whole **Generous Qur'an** is a guiding force. The authors have deliberately put the above verses in this book several times, because we believe vehemently that they explain to all humanity what the Islamic paradigm is all about. All of the **Generous Qur'an** is full of Light, pearls and jewels. Therefore, we are not constructing something new. We are only asserting what is there.

It would be next to impossible to explain the infinite dimensions of this paradigm of the contextual belief of Islam, because **ALLAH** (*subhanahu wa ta'ala*) has already explained it in the **Generous Qur'an**. According to the **Generous Qur'an**, the first step any human being must follow in order to have the proper belief is to strip the individual self of skepticism and doubt. The next step is for the individual to develop certainty. Through the teaching of Islam as a *modus operandi* and *modus vivendi*, and with the guidance of **ALLAH** (*subhanahu wa ta'ala*), the person could reach this stage of certainty. Making submission means that a person will be transformed from a lower, mundane human estate that is governed by deviation, to a higher, divinely-oriented human estate governed by the Divine Law. At that point he or she starts to *see*. Seeing is a result of this divinely-ordained Law. This is why the above verses of *Surah Al-Baqqara* have infinite oceans. We want the reader to read these verses, because they compose for us in a simple way what the Islamic paradigm is.

166

The Arabic, Qur'anic and Islamic Paradigm:
Light, Jewels and Pearls

Chapter VI. An Islamic Paradigm for Belief

Within this understanding, we are trying to focus on some concepts that **ALLAH** (*subhanahu wa ta'ala*) has explicitly indicated as variables and conceptual apparati which might play a role in explaining the infinite Light, jewels, pearls and oceans of the Islamic paradigm for belief. Again, the authors are not building anything, but rather asserting what is already there. Only **ALLAH** (*subhanahu wa ta'ala*) knows best, and we accept our human limitations. At this juncture of the analysis, the focus will be on certain select concepts that the above five *ayat* (verses) in *Surah Al-Baqqara* indicate. One of these is the belief in the unseen. The next is *salaat*. This exposé will focus in detail on these, though the *ayat* are already clear to the true believer. One of the main concepts of these *ayat* is that the true believer, in order to understand the **Generous Qur'an** as a guiding force, must have *taqwa* (piety)

Those who have *taqwa* are first supposed to believe in the unseen. What is the relationship between belief and the unseen? **ALLAH** (*subhanahu wa ta'ala*) ordered us to develop a strong belief. The issue at hand, however, is not to develop strong belief in the physical, apparent dimension of that which can be seen by the human faculties, because what humans see with human faculties is the encapsulation of certain objects within the framework of the illusionary interplay between space and time. Whatever one sees in one's physical eye is no more than images, which are illusions. Many people try to believe in something that is an illusion. They hold on to goals like getting a Ph.D., a million dollars, or a mansion, etc. Even when a person obtains those things, however, he will not be at rest. Prior to obtaining these transitional, contemporaneous and illusionary goals, one tends to think that peace, tranquility and satisfaction will come as a result of their fulfillment. The individual tries to take refuge in these illusionary goals. When he

167

acquires them, however, he will suffer from cognitive dissonance, which is the incongruity between expectations and empirical reality. Therefore, the physically visible goals of the mundane eye do not provide the peace, security and tranquility that the individual seeks. **ALLAH** (*subhanahu wa ta'ala*) uses the word *iman* (belief) whose root is *amn*, which means peace, security and tranquility. The visible, seen dimension of the physical world, *pari passu* the mundane world, can never fulfill the conceptual and verbatim meaning of the word *amn*, which is peace and security. That is because the life of this world is deceptive.[1]

****

SURAH III (3) *The Family of 'Imran*

14. Beautified for mankind is love of the joys (that come) from women and offspring, and stored-up heaps of gold and silver, and horses branded (with their mark), and cattle and land. That is comfort of the life of the world. Allah! With Him is a more excellent abode.

زُيِّنَ لِلنَّاسِ حُبُّ الشَّهَوَٰتِ مِنَ النِّسَآءِ وَالْبَنِينَ وَالْقَنَاطِيرِ الْمُقَنْطَرَةِ مِنَ الذَّهَبِ وَالْفِضَّةِ وَالْخَيْلِ الْمُسَوَّمَةِ وَالْأَنْعَامِ وَالْحَرْثِ ذَٰلِكَ مَتَاعُ الْحَيَوٰةِ الدُّنْيَا وَاللَّهُ عِنْدَهُ حُسْنُ الْمَآبِ ﴿٤﴾

III *Surah Ali-'Imran*, **The Generous Qur'an** 3:14

****

168

****

SURAH LVII (57) *Iron*

20.   Know that the life of this world is only play, and idle talk, and pageantry, and boasting among you, and rivalry in respect of wealth and children; as the likeness of vegetation after rain, whereof the growth is pleasing to the husbandman, but afterward it drieth up and thou seest it turning yellow, then it becometh straw. And in the Hereafter there is grievous punishment, and (also) forgiveness from Allah and His good pleasure, whereas the life of the world is but matter of illusion.

21.   Race one with another for forgiveness from your Lord and a Garden whereof the breadth is as the breadth of the heavens and the earth, which is in store for those who believe in Allah and His messengers. Such is the bounty of Allah, which He bestoweth upon whim He will, and Allah is of Infinite bounty.

اِعْلَمُوٓا اَنَّمَا الْحَيٰوةُ الدُّنْيَا لَعِبٌ وَّلَهْوٌ وَّزِينَةٌ وَّ تَفَاخُرٌ بَيْنَكُمْ وَتَكَاثُرٌ فِي الْاَمْوَالِ وَالْاَوْلَادِ كَمَثَلِ غَيْثٍ اَعْجَبَ الْكُفَّارَ نَبَاتُهٗ ثُمَّ يَهِيْجُ فَتَرٰىهُ مُصْفَرًّا ثُمَّ يَكُوْنُ حُطَامًا وَفِي الْاٰخِرَةِ عَذَابٌ شَدِيْدٌ وَّمَغْفِرَةٌ مِّنَ اللّٰهِ وَرِضْوَانٌ وَمَا الْحَيٰوةُ الدُّنْيَا اِلَّا مَتَاعُ الْغُرُوْرِ ۝

سَابِقُوٓا اِلٰى مَغْفِرَةٍ مِّنْ رَّبِّكُمْ وَجَنَّةٍ عَرْضُهَا كَعَرْضِ السَّمَاءِ وَالْاَرْضِ اُعِدَّتْ لِلَّذِيْنَ اٰمَنُوْا بِاللّٰهِ وَرُسُلِهٖ ذٰلِكَ فَضْلُ اللّٰهِ يُؤْتِيْهِ مَنْ يَّشَاءُ وَاللّٰهُ ذُو الْفَضْلِ الْعَظِيْمِ ۝

LVII *Surah Al-Hadid*, **The Generous Qur'an** 57:20-21

****

169

Chapter VI. An Islamic Paradigm for Belief

ALLAH (*subhanahu wa ta'ala*) wants His people to believe in the real world, not the illusionary world, because the illusionary world is entropic and can never fulfill the expectations of the individual. **ALLAH** (*subhanahu wa ta'ala*) wants us to believe in Him and what He has ordained as *Al-Ghayb* (the unseen), such as the Day of Judgement, the Life Hereafter, Paradise and Hell, the Angels, the Spirit, etc. All of these *are* the real world. However, the encapsulated mind of the mundane world cannot comprehend because there is a *barzakh*, an invisible realm which serves like a barrier that the non-believers cannot transgress. If human beings want to believe in **ALLAH** (*subhanahu wa ta'ala*), they must overcome their obsession with the mundane, physical world, because it is no more than an illusion, and a test which has to be overcome.[2]

Though the human faculties cannot see the unseen, "real", world, this does not imply the negation of that world. What it indicates is the limitation of human faculties in their ability to totally comprehend the world beyond. What is clear is that the world beyond has been there all along. It is man's destiny to "fall" and be put in a world where he is encapsulated by the illusionary interplay between space and time. This journey is no more than a momentary leave of absence from the real world where peace, tranquility and security constitute the perpetual *modus operandi* and *modus vivendi*. What is an illusion is the "leave of absence", and this is why most of the true believers don't feel at home in this mundane, physical, visible and entropic world. The true believers want to go back home. That is to say, they want to go from the physically visible world back to the world beyond. While they are

Chapter VI. An Islamic Paradigm for Belief

living in this physical, entropic, visible, illusionary world, however, they live according to the *modus operandi* and *modus vivendi* of the invisible world by following the Straight Path. Becoming the embodiment of the Straight Path in the visible, mundane world is itself the journey back to the world beyond.[3]

While the true believers are in the mundane world, they are occupied totally with the invisible world. Therefore, the invisible world, to the true believer and the truly conscious, is a full time job. This is because in reality there are not two worlds; there is only one world. The mundane world is only a stop-over or a testing ground to distinguish between those who will be the occupants of Hell and those who will be the occupants of Heaven, neither of which are visible at this point in time, but whose existence is real. This is why we have to believe in the existence of Heaven and Hell, and try to do what is good all the time prior to our individual deaths. No one knows when a person is going to die except **ALLAH** (*subhanahu wa ta'ala*). Our good deeds in this life are the seeds which will grow in the next life. The true believer, like a good farmer. plants something here that he can harvest there, because we are just going back to the world beyond where we came from. A conscious person plants here in the anticipation that when he goes back he will harvest there, where he really belongs.

The only person who can understand this is one whose self is tranquil here, meaning that he really went through self-annihilation, and as a result was able to overcome the illusionary interplay between space and time. Thus he was able to bury arrogance and selfishness, and be at peace with himself. That tranquil self will go back to where it came from. The heart is the

171

guide of the true believer, because in ultimate reality, there are not two worlds but only one.

****

<u>SURAH LXXXIX (89)</u> *The Dawn*

27. But ah! thou soul at peace!

28. Return unto thy Lord, content in His good pleasure!

29. Enter thou among My bondmen!

30. Enter thou My Garden!

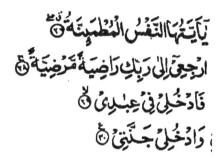

LXXXIX *Surah Fajr*, **The Generous Qur'an** 89:27-30

****

There really are no two worlds; there is only one. Those who are bogged down with illusion, and thereby become perplexed, arrogant and selfish, did not achieve the status of real submission. They were on a mundane trip or a fad in which they became the embodiment of self-glorification. Self-glorification makes the individual to be a discontented hustler. That in itself means that he is trapped within a cocoon of hypocrisy which makes his human estate to be something other than a contented self. This means that

172

he is not pleased with himself. What he is here in the mundane, he will be there in the beyond. If he is disgusted in this world, he is disgusted there. If makes himself to be in Hell here, he is sure to be in Hell there. By the same token, if he really surrenders and comes to the glimpse that he is happy here, and comes to achieve tranquility, he will be tranquil there. Simply put, there are no two worlds. What you are here, you become there.[4]

Again, at this level, it is imperative to understand that in reality, there are not two worlds. There is only one world. Some people might differentiate between the mundane and the beyond, but the mundane has only relative existence, not authentic existence.[5] The mundane is relative because it is a short span of time in comparison to the beyond, which is eternal. In actuality it is a prelude to the beyond, so a truly conscious person tries to come to grips with the reality that he should achieve tranquility in this world. That can never be achieved through self-glorification or arrogance. But it can be achieved through a total submission to **ALLAH** (*subhanahu wa ta'ala*) and through becoming the embodiment of His Laws. These Laws are designed to put the individual under the jurisdiction of the Supreme, **ALLAH** (*subhanahu wa ta'ala*). Thereby, the individual is not governed by dualistic sets of rules or ethics, with one set for his private and one for his public realm, or one for his hidden and one for his apparent realm. An individual who makes submission to **ALLAH** (*subhanahu wa ta'ala*) knows that **ALLAH** (*subhanahu wa ta'ala*) knows what the eye hides. He knows that **ALLAH** (*subhanahu wa ta'ala*) invades and navigates through the chest and the heart. At that level a conscious, authentic Muslim comes to strip himself of hypocrisy and cease the show-business of trying to convey

173

something that he is not. People tend to try to convey this only because their god is something that it is not.

When the individual as a true Muslim becomes the practitioner of the Law of **ALLAH** (*subhanahu wa ta'ala*), he becomes happy.[6] He is happy and has nothing to worry about. This means that this authentic Muslim has achieved a very high status in the eyes of **ALLAH** (*subhanahu wa ta'ala*), because he made himself to be at the lowest of the low in the mundane. The individual prostrates in order to indicate that he is nothing, and that he is glorifying **ALLAH** (*subhanahu wa ta'ala*) physically by bowing to Him. The lower he goes, the more he is at a higher status in **ALLAH's** (*subhanahu wa ta'ala*) eyes. **ALLAH** (*subhanahu wa ta'ala*) is the Most High, and the slave is closest to Him when he is bowing. The slave is bowing with joy. That joy makes his self to be tranquil.

A person whose heart is blind in this world will be blind in the next world, and even more deviant. He will be unable to see, though his eyes are open. On the Day of Judgement, he will be astonished as to why he has been aggregated with those who are blind. The **Generous Qur'an** indicates that on that Day, he will be reminded that the verses and signs of **ALLAH** (*subhanahu wa ta'ala*) came to him and he forgot them and tried to avoid them. Because he forgot and tried to avoid them in the mundane world, he will be among the forgotten on the Day of Judgement. That is to say that in the mundane world, he was not the embodiment of the **Generous Qur'an** and the *Shari'atu* **ALLAH** (*subhanahu wa ta'ala*). By the same token, those individuals in whose hearts **ALLAH** (*subhanahu wa ta'ala*) put Light, whose hearts **ALLAH** (*subhanahu wa ta'ala*) has not sealed with darkness, do their best to be the

174

embodiment of the Word of **ALLAH** (*subhanahu wa ta'ala*), the *Shari'ah*, in this mundane world. This means that they become truly conscious, and as a result, they *see* the Word of **ALLAH** (*subhanahu wa ta'ala*), *hear* it and *practice* it in their private realm and their public realm, in their hidden and outward realms. These individuals are *seeing* individuals, so they will be aggregated on the Day of Judgement with those who see, who are the embodiment of the Law of **ALLAH** (*subhanahu wa ta'ala*).[7]

This leads us to understand that *Tawhid* means the unity of belief and action, and consequently happiness in both this world and the next world. These "two" relative worlds are governed by the Law of **ALLAH** (*subhanahu wa ta'ala*). A truely conscious person prepares here for his existence there. He plants here and harvests both here and there. He is really doing everything for **ALLAH** (*subhanahu wa ta'ala*). He is at a stage of total surrender and submission to Him. At that point, **ALLAH** (*subhanahu wa ta'ala*) calls to him, "come back where you have been, blessed, content and in good pleasure, and enter among My servants, enter My Garden".

This simply means that man has been on a temporary leave of absence in the anticipation of returning to where he belongs. This is why **ALLAH** (*subhanahu wa ta'ala*) associates belief with the unseen. It is in order to make His people believe in **ALLAH** (*subhanahu wa ta'ala*) first and foremost. This is the Straight Path, which leads them to the real yet unseen, invisible world, in the anticipation of their journey back to **ALLAH** (*subhanahu wa ta'ala*), Whom no human consciousness can encompass.

The Secret of *Salaat*

* *

<u>SURAH XXIX (29)</u> *The Spider*

45. Recite that which hath been inspired in thee of the Scripture, and establish worship.   Lo! worship preserveth from lewdness and iniquity, but verily remembrance of Allah is more important.   And Allah knoweth what ye do.

أُتْلُ مَآ أُوحِىَ إِلَيْكَ مِنَ الْكِتَبِ وَأَقِمِ الصَّلَوٰةَ إِنَّ الصَّلَوٰةَ تَنْهَى عَنِ الْفَحْشَآءِ وَالْمُنْكَرِ وَلَذِكْرُ اللَّهِ أَكْبَرُ وَاللَّهُ يَعْلَمُ مَا تَصْنَعُونَ ۝

XXIX *Surah Al-'Ankabut,* **The Generous Qur'an** 29:45

* *

In their chronological expression, the first five *ayat* in *Surah Al-Baqqara,* quoted at the beginning of this chapter, must be understood as one unit. Nevertheless, each *ayah* has a contextual relationship to the other *ayat*. Therefore, each *ayah* becomes the inward and outward linkage to the one preceding it and the one following it.   This isomorphically creates a citadel of meaning which is integrated to constitute a total, complete way.   This way

176

delineates a *modus operandi* and a *modus vivendi* to the final touch, in the anticipation of that those who follow it will live according to Straightness. This Straightness can be no other than the Way which has been ordained by **ALLAH** (*subhanahu wa ta'ala*). If one believes in **ALLAH** (*subhanahu wa ta'ala*) and makes submission to Him that is the key to all success. If one believes in **ALLAH** (*subhanahu wa ta'ala*), one has to become the embodiment of **ALLAH's** (*subhanahu wa ta'ala*) Way as He delineated it.

After having mentioned belief in the unseen, **ALLAH** (*subhanahu wa ta'ala*) asserts that one must practice the *salaat* (the five daily prayers). *Salaat* is one of the pillars of Islam, and constitutes the main stake for each individual's practice of Islam. When a person performs *salaat,* as **ALLAH** (*subhanahu wa ta'ala*) ordained and the **Prophet Muhammad** (*prayers and peace of* **ALLAH** *be upon him*) showed us, this means that he has established the *Din* (way of life) of Islam. It is like a tent which has the main pole and pillar in the middle. Everything else goes around it and is linked to it, establishing a milieu of homeostasis. When a person performs *salaat*, he is simultaneously performing, in part, all the other pillars of Islam in one way or another. This is why **ALLAH** (*subhanahu wa ta'ala*) makes *salaat* an obligation for every individual regardless of his or her human condition or capability. It makes sense that **ALLAH** (*subhanahu wa ta'ala*) made the order for *salaat* to follow the order to believe in the unseen.

ALLAH (*subhanahu wa ta'ala*) ordered that *salaat* be done in the visible world. It's reward and ramifications are for the visible world as well as the invisible world. Thereby, *salaat* becomes the linkage between the mundane world and the world beyond; i.e. between the visible world and the invisible world, the seen world

177

and the unseen world. It is imperative to understand that the *salaat* (*pari passu* prayers) is a linkage between two worlds or realms. The performer of the *salaat* constitutes the inward and outward linkage between the two realms. The verbatim root of the term *salaat* in Arabic means, first, to burn. Burning in this sense implies ironing and stretching out crookedness, the result of which is straightness and readiness. The second verbatim root of *salaat* is linkage. It has many other meanings as well.[8]

The Purifying Fire of *Salaat*

****

SURAH LXXXIV (84) *The Sundering*

12. And be thrown to scorching fire. تَيَصْلَىٰ سَعِيْرًاۢ ۞

LXXXIV *Surah Al-Inshiqaq*, **The Generous Qur'an** 84:12

****

As mentioned, one of the meanings of the word *salaat* in Arabic comes from its root *sala*, which means to burn by fire or to iron. In *Surah Al-Lail, ayah* 15, **ALLAH** (*subhanahu wa ta'ala*) uses the term *yaslaha* ("to be ironed"). It is repeated in *Surah Inshiqaq*,

178

ayah 12: *wa yasla sa'eeran* ("he will be ironed by fire"). It is again repeated in *Surah Lahab, ayah* 3: *sayasla naran* (he will be burned by fire). It is a mystery how, when **ALLAH** (*subhanahu wa ta'ala*) uses a word, it fulfills all its verbatim and conceptual meaning.

When a person wants to perform *salaat* (the prayers), something is burning in him. The question becomes what is burning? When one stands up to perform *salaat,* he is aggregating all of his consciousnesss and trying his best to direct himself towards the Straight Way because he is worshipping **ALLAH** (*subhanahu wa ta'ala).* If he is committed to **ALLAH** (*subhanahu wa ta'ala),* he should try his best not to let anything take his attention away during the *salaat* . He cannot direct his face, intentions and thoughts toward **ALLAH** (*subhanahu wa ta'ala),* focusing on the *ka'aba* in *Makkah Al-Mukerramah* (The House of God in Mecca) while he is preoccupied with thoughts of his business, family, sex or anything else. If he believes in **ALLAH** (*subhanahu wa ta'ala),* he should only be the slave of **ALLAH** (*subhanahu wa ta'ala),* not the slave of his neurotic and psychotic mundane feelings, thoughts and activities. A human can only be the slave of one master, not two.[9]

Though he wants to perform *salaat* and be in the Straight Way, it is usually the case that *Shaytan* (Satan) tries to stand in his way. *Shaytan* wants to lure him from the Straight Way and starts to whisper to him to make him think of things other than **ALLAH** (*subhanahu wa ta'ala),* such as his business, his children, sex, etc. While the individual is performing *salaat* he is, in actuality, thinking of something other than **ALLAH** (*subhanahu wa ta'ala).* Therefore, he is in two worlds simultaneously: the Straight Way and the deviant, *Shaytanic* way. He himself becomes the linkage between them. He is therefore either not doing *salaat,* or else he is

179

doing *salaat* in the lowest degree. If he wants to really do *salaat* in the right and straight way, he has to burn the *Shaytanic* way from his path and from his lower psychotic, neurotic self which has been lured by *Shaytan*. *Shaytan* tries to capture one's attention, glorify it and model it after an illusionary world of make-believe. This is why the *Shaytanic* way must be burned, so that instead of being preoccupied with the world of make-believe, the person will be occupied with the remembrance of **ALLAH** (*subhanahu wa ta'ala*) and the real world. Then, nothing else could capture or lure his attention. At that point he is really performing the prayers, *pari passu* the *salaat*, correctly.[10]

****

SURAH VII (7) *The Heights*

16. He [Shaytan] said: Now, because Thou hast sent me astray, verily I shall lurk in ambush for them on Thy Right Path.

قَالَ فَبِمَا أَغْوَيْتَنِي لَأَقْعُدَنَّ لَهُمْ صِرَاطَكَ الْمُسْتَقِيمَ ۞

17. Then I shall come upon them from before them and from behind them and from their right hands and from their left hands, and Thou wilt not find most of them beholden (unto Thee).

ثُمَّ لَآتِيَنَّهُم مِّنۢ بَيْنِ أَيْدِيهِمْ وَمِنْ خَلْفِهِمْ وَعَنْ أَيْمَانِهِمْ وَعَن شَمَآئِلِهِمْ وَلَا تَجِدُ أَكْثَرَهُمْ شَاكِرِينَ ۞

VII *Surah Al-A'raf*, **The Generous Qur'an** 7:16-17

****

180

When people try to stand up in the straight way to do *salaat* (prayers), *Shaytan* intensifies his work. He tries to approach them and distract them from "between their hands" in the front, from their backs, from their right sides and from their left sides. Therefore, *Shaytan* tries to surround man from almost all sides. Those whom *Shaytan* has lured and whose attention he has captured have been extracted from the Straight Path of **ALLAH** (*subhanahu wa ta'ala*) and been entrapped by the deviant path of *Shaytan* . They are not really doing *salaat* at its highest level of performance. *Salaat* at this dimension becomes a linkage to the deviant way, not a linkage to **ALLAH's** (*subhanahu wa ta'ala*) Way. The individual has become bogged down with the whispering of *Shaytan*. This may be only a stage in which the person is cleansed as a prelude to a true linkage to **ALLAH** (*subhanahu wa ta'ala*).

This performance of *Shaytan* is almost identical to his performance with our original parents in paradise, Adam (*peace be upon him*) and his spouse. *Shaytan* successfully lured and manipulated them when he appeared to them as "an advisor". He was the original cause of their displacement from paradise. However, our original parents confessed their error, which was that they should have only listened to and become the embodiment of the Word of **ALLAH** (*subhanahu wa ta'ala*), without any doubts or second thoughts, without any modification and without any conceptual deviation or reinterpretation. They should have adhered to the verbatim order of the Word of **ALLAH** (*subhanahu wa ta'ala*), implemented and lived it in *praxis,* and continuously remembered the Word as it was ordained, regardless of any kind of alternative or advice whispered to them by *Shaytan* . In other words, since the Word of **ALLAH** (*subhanahu wa ta'ala*) has come

181

to mankind, especially when one is praying, one should do his best not to hear anything else.[11]

Our parents gave *Shaytan* the forum within which he could express himself. This means that they allowed him into themselves, their domain and their lives. *Shaytan* was the cause of their displacement from Heaven to earth for a short period of time. This is why **ALLAH** (*subhanahu wa ta'ala*), through His *Shari'ah*, explicitly indicated that a Muslim should not come close to the road that leads to deviation, alcoholism, crime, adultery, etc. The forum of *Shaytan* is an apparatus legalized and licensed through satanic statism. It is satanic statism that gives licences to sell alcohol, drugs, prostituted and other commercial sex, etc. *Shaytan* gets this forum under the pretense of "human rights", liberalism, sexual permissiveness, etc.[12] A true Muslim should not associate himself with people involved in this kind of forum.

Individuals often become trapped between a variety of groups and pairs. Sometimes the individual wants to please one group, another time he wants to please another group. Each of these groups has its own value system that is something other than Islam. To a certain extent, this way is based on satanic values. Some Muslims would like to be apologetic toward the satanic way, saying "we are OK and you are OK". Thereby, they associate themselves with these satanic pairs, who have their own *salaat*, which is booze, women, drugs, and all the prohibited things. This satanic performance of *salaat* is concealed under the slogans of liberalism and modernity, and so on.

Some hypocritical, self-styled Muslims like to make accommodations between satanic ways and Islam, and sway between two clusters of peer groups. In their behavior they sway

182

back and forth. They would like to accommodate Muslims, so they say "we pray and come to the mosque". When they go back to their deviant group, they try to accommodate members of the latter by drinking alcohol, etc., just in the anticipation of avoiding conflict or embarassment, because they feel weak inside. If they were really Muslims, they would stand in the midst of these deviant, weak people who have been engulfed by *Shaytan*, and try to therapeutically explain to these people that there is hope if they would leave this deviation, which is unhealthy and produces no more than sickness and straying. A true Muslim should do his best not to be in the presence of satanic apparatus. He should avoid giving *Shaytan* a forum in which to be heard and from which to perform his glimmering technique, using various kinds of whisperings, tricks and concealments. The latter might include the drinking of alcohol and all other kinds of prohibited deviation. It is assured that those who adhere to the call of *Shaytan* have been caused by **ALLAH** (*subhanahu wa ta'ala*) to go astray, and there will be no way found for them.[13]

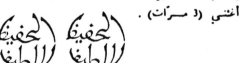

183

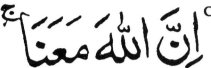 

Salaat vis-á-vis the *Shaytanic* Forum

* *

SURAH VII (7) *The Heights*

27. O Children of Adam! Let not Satan seduce you as he caused your (first) parents to go forth from the Garden and tore off from them their robe (of innocence) that he might manifest their shame to them. Lo! he seeth you, he and his tribe, from whence ye see him not. Lo! We have made the devils protecting friends for those who believe not.

يَٰبَنِىٓ ءَادَمَ لَا يَفْتِنَنَّكُمُ ٱلشَّيْطَٰنُ كَمَآ أَخْرَجَ أَبَوَيْكُم مِّنَ ٱلْجَنَّةِ يَنزِعُ عَنْهُمَا لِبَاسَهُمَا لِيُرِيَهُمَا سَوْءَٰتِهِمَآ إِنَّهُۥ يَرَىٰكُمْ هُوَ وَقَبِيلُهُۥ مِنْ حَيْثُ لَا تَرَوْنَهُمْ إِنَّا جَعَلْنَا ٱلشَّيَٰطِينَ أَوْلِيَآءَ لِلَّذِينَ لَا يُؤْمِنُونَ ۝

VII *Surah Al-A'raf*, **The Generous Qur'an** 7:27

* *

Shaytan is desperately looking for a niche in which he can first conceal himself, then secure a forum from which to be heard. He does this through people who are deviant in their behavior. He tries to associate himself with them, under the pretense of humanism, moderation, majority rule, minority rights, liberation, or whatever seasonal slogans that happen to be in vogue. Therefore, adherence to *Shaytan* means to listen to him, and to

184

allow him to perform a detrimental linkage from the straight way to the deviant way. Some people physically perform *salaat* while allowing *Shaytan* to whisper in their ears, and to be in their presence from almost all directions. If they listen to him, he will bait, lure and engulf them, with the result that an individual could reach a point of no return, left naked as after a violent storm, with no refuge of any kind. Under such conditions, one is outwardly and physically going through the movements of *salaat* while he is in actuality being kidnapped and displaced from the real, straight world to the illusionary world of make-believe.[14]

This is why **ALLAH** (*subhanahu wa ta'ala*) warns us not to make the same errors as our original parents did by letting *Shaytan* beguile and seduce us and put us off guard by just listening to him and giving him a forum for our attention. When a person wants to make *salaat*, he has to understand that it is something like devotion to **ALLAH** (*subhanahu wa ta'ala*) and he should try his best not to be reluctant, perplexed, ostentatious, or lazy, because he is becoming swayed between a variation of groups, one group *vis-á-vis* the other. Thereby his performance of *salaat* was a linkage, not to **ALLAH** (*subhanahu wa ta'ala*), but between two groups. That is the first step of deviation. As a result, he comes to be in the realm of the hypocrites. This means, simply put, that he really didn't do *salaat*.

There is no real *salaat* while there is deviation. The real way to do *salaat* is to burn and uproot the *Shaytanic* way, values and deviation which make one obsessed with the glorification of the self, making that self preoccupied with mundane, deviant and crooked things. What has to happen is that all deviation, insincerity, crookedness, laziness, dullness, denseness and

185

weightiness has to be burned away and ironed out of the self. The self has to be straight. After it has been ironed and cleansed, it has prepared itself to have communion with the Word of **ALLAH** - God (*subhanahu wa ta'ala*) because **ALLAH** (*subhanahu wa ta'ala*) ordered us to have tranquility, peace, total surrender, commitment and congeniality when we make *salaat* . Therefore, a person who does the *salaat* right will seek rest *in* it, not *from* it. That is when a person finds happiness in the *salaat* because there is no other higher value in the world than to respond to the call of **ALLAH** (*subhanahu wa ta'ala*) by performing *salaat* , reciting His Words and making total submission by giving all one's consciousness to **ALLAH** (*subhanahu wa ta'ala*), Who has created him out of nothingness. This is why a person has to iron himself out and not take *salaat* lightly as a show, game or role-playing. After doing this, the *salaat* becomes a linkage to the Divine and to the world beyond.[15]

186

وَمَا تَوْفِيقِي إِلَّا بِاللَّهِ عَلَيْهِ تَوَكَّلْتُ وَإِلَيْهِ أُنِيبُ

****

SURAH IV (4) *Women*

142.   Lo! the hypocrites seek to beguile Allah, but it is Allah who beguileth them. When they stand up to worship they perform it languidly and to be seen of men, and are mindful of Allah but little;

143.   Swaying between this (and that), (belonging) neither to these nor to those. He whom Allah causeth to go astray, thou (O Muhammad) wilt not find a way for him:

إِنَّ الْمُنَافِقِينَ يُخَادِعُونَ اللَّهَ وَهُوَ خَادِعُهُمْ وَإِذَا قَامُوا إِلَى الصَّلَاةِ قَامُوا كُسَالَى يُرَاؤُونَ النَّاسَ وَلَا يَذْكُرُونَ اللَّهَ إِلَّا قَلِيلًا ۝

مُذَبْذَبِينَ بَيْنَ ذَلِكَ لَا إِلَى هَؤُلَاءِ وَلَا إِلَى هَؤُلَاءِ وَمَن يُضْلِلِ اللَّهُ فَلَن تَجِدَ لَهُ سَبِيلًا ۝

IV *Surah Al-Nisaa*, **The Generous Qur'an** 4:142-143

****

قال له رسول الله ــ صلى الله عليه وسلم ــ : « لا تسأل مخلوقا مثلك ولكن اعلمك كلمات ادع بها الله ، فإنها تجلب الرزق . فقل كل يوم : « اللهم اثبت في قلبي رجاءك ، واقطع رجائي عمن سواك ، حتى لا أرجو أحدا غيرك » . اللهم وما ضعفت عنه قوتي وقصر عنه عملي ولم تبلغه مسألتي ولم يجر على لساني ما أعطيت أحدا من الأولين والآخرين ، فخصني وآتني به يا رب العالمين » .

اِنَّ اللّهَ مَعَنَا   اِنَّ اللّهَ مَعَنَا   A Continuous Integrative *Praxis*   اِنَّ اللّهَ مَعَنَا

****

SURAH II (2) *The Cow*

238. Be guardians of your prayers,
and of the midmost prayer, and stand
up with devotion to Allah.

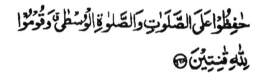

II *Surah Al-Baqqara* , The Generous Qur'an 2:238

****

In Islam there are five (an odd number) daily *salaat*. It is
imperative to understand why **ALLAH** (*subhanahu wa ta'ala*)
ordained five *salaat* and spread them throughout the whole day, as
a requirement (*fard*).[16] Throughout the whole day a person has to
live the teaching of *salaat* in his *praxis*. Each of the five *salaat* is
considered to be a middle *salaat* because it is a linkage between the
one prior to and the one after it. The period in between each *salaat*
is a linkage betwen two *salaats*, during which the one who prays
should preserve, in his *praxis*, what he is trying to achieve in his
salaat. That is to say, the noon prayer is a linkage between the
morning and afternoon prayers. The period between morning and
noon prayer is also a linkage between these two prayers, and the
praxis of one's *modus operandi* and *modus vivendi* ought to be

188

the embodiment of the teaching (*pari passu* the straight path) of these two prayers. The *asr*, (afternoon) prayer is also a middle prayer, because it is a linkage between noon and sunset prayer. Again, the period between noon and afternoon prayers is a linkage between these two prayers.

In Islam, there is no dualism.[17] Therefore, what has been pursued during two prayers should also be pursued during the period of time in between these two prayers. Islam is a unity between belief and action, which produces real peace for the individual. What you worship in your prayer, you practice every day of your life. This is also true for sunset (*maghrib*) prayer, night (*'isha*) prayer and morning (*fajr*) prayer because all of them are a "middle" prayer or linkage. ALLAH (*subhanahu wa ta'ala*) ordered us to preserve the middle prayer and live in accordance with His Way during the time linkages between every prayer. Therefore, true Muslims live on the straight path, worshipping ALLAH (*subhanahu wa ta'ala*) and doing salaat all day and all night according to the teaching of the **Generous Qur'an**.

189

وَمَا تَوْفِيقِى إِلَّا بِاللَّهِ عَلَيْهِ تَوَكَّلْتُ وَإِلَيْهِ أُنِيبُ

The Arabic, Qur'anic and Islamic Paradigm:
Light, Jewels and Pearls

Chapter VI. An Islamic Paradigm for Belief

✦✦

SURAH XVII (17) *The Night Journey*

78. Establish worship at the going down of the sun until the dark of night, and (the recital of) the Qur'an at dawn. Lo! (the recital) of the Qur'an at dawn is ever witnessed.

79. And some part of the night awake for it, a largess for thee. It may be that thy Lord wil raise thee to a praised estate.

أَقِمِ الصَّلَوٰةَ لِدُلُوكِ الشَّمْسِ إِلَىٰ غَسَقِ الَّيْلِ وَقُرْآنَ الْفَجْرِ إِنَّ قُرْآنَ الْفَجْرِ كَانَ مَشْهُودًا ۩ وَمِنَ الَّيْلِ فَتَهَجَّدْ بِهِ نَافِلَةً لَّكَ عَسَىٰ أَن يَبْعَثَكَ رَبُّكَ مَقَامًا مَّحْمُودًا ۩

XVII *Surah Al-Israa'*, **The Generous Qur'an** 17:78-79

✦✦

ALLAH (*subhanahu wa ta'ala*) ordered man to establish regular prayers also at sunset, night, deep into the night and in the morning. One should also read the **Generous Qur'an** at the time of the early morning prayer, because this carries a great testimony leading to reward. The **Prophet Muhammad** (*prayers and peace of* **ALLAH** *be upon him*) also used to pray extra prayers after midnight called *Tahajjud*. He established a precedent in order to convey a message to humankind in general and to the true believers. Therefore, **ALLAH** (*subhanahu wa ta'ala*) wants us to establish regular prayer at the two ends of the day, to preserve every "middle prayer" and practice our prayer during the interrim according to the

190

straight path. He wants us also to pray during the night, and late night. This means we have to be in prayers all the time and carry our prayers to every dimension of life.

ALLAH (*subhanahu wa ta'ala*) created a perfect world which encompasses everything to serve mankind. He also ordained the wealth of each human so that they could worship only ALLAH (*subhanahu wa ta'ala*) in every dimension and not be preoccupied with any trivial things such as worshipping something other than ALLAH (*subhanahu wa ta'ala*) which could neither benefit nor harm them. This is why ALLAH (*subhanahu wa ta'ala*) explicitly said that He created humans and the *jinn* only to worship ALLAH (*subhanahu wa ta'ala*) all their lives and to live according to His Law.[18]

****

SURAH LI (51) *The Winnowing*
Winds

56.   I created the jinn and humankind only that they might worship Me.

57. I seek no livelihood from them, nor do I ask that they should feed Me.

58. Lo! Allah! He it is that giveth livelihood, the Lord of Unbreakable might.

وَمَاخَلَقْتُ الْجِنَّ وَالْإِنْسَ إِلَّا لِيَعْبُدُونِ ۝
مَآ أُرِيدُ مِنْهُم مِّن رِّزْقٍ وَمَآ أُرِيدُ أَن يُطْعِمُونِ ۝
إِنَّ اللَّهَ هُوَ الرَّزَّاقُ ذُو الْقُوَّةِ الْمَتِينُ ۝

LI *Surah Al-Thariyat*, **The Generous Qur'an** 51:56-58

****

191

To live according to **ALLAH's** (*subhanahu wa ta'ala*) rules means to take the individual away from deviation and remind him constantly of the straight way. This is why there is physical and periodical performance of the *salaat* in order to teach and constantly remind the individual how to be straight by fearing **ALLAH** (*subhanahu wa ta'ala*) Who is observing and recording every outer and inner dimension of that individual's life. A person cannot be drunk or drugged while he is doing *salaat* or he won't know what he is saying. Because the five *salaat* come one after the other throughout the day, a person would not have time to drink alcohol or take drugs and be sober in time for the next prayer. This is why **ALLAH** (*subhanahu wa ta'ala*) prohibitted mind-befoggling substances such as alcohol and drugs.[19] They are the embodiment of *Shaytan's* way.

****

SURAH IV (4) *Women*

43. O ye who believe! Draw not near unto prayer when ye are drunken, till ye know that which ye utter, nor when ye are polluted save when journeying upon the road, till ye have bathed. And if ye be ill, or on a journey, or one of you touched women, and ye find not water, then go to high clean soil and rub your faces and your hands (therewith).   Lo! Allah is Benign, Forgiving.

يَٰٓأَيُّهَا ٱلَّذِينَ ءَامَنُوا۟ لَا تَقْرَبُوا۟ ٱلصَّلَوٰةَ وَأَنتُمْ سُكَٰرَىٰ حَتَّىٰ تَعْلَمُوا۟ مَا تَقُولُونَ وَلَا جُنُبًا إِلَّا عَابِرِى سَبِيلٍ حَتَّىٰ تَغْتَسِلُوا۟ وَإِن كُنتُم مَّرْضَىٰٓ أَوْ عَلَىٰ سَفَرٍ أَوْ جَآءَ أَحَدٌ مِّنكُم مِّنَ ٱلْغَآئِطِ أَوْ لَٰمَسْتُمُ ٱلنِّسَآءَ فَلَمْ تَجِدُوا۟ مَآءً فَتَيَمَّمُوا۟ صَعِيدًا طَيِّبًا فَٱمْسَحُوا۟ بِوُجُوهِكُمْ وَأَيْدِيكُمْ إِنَّ ٱللَّهَ كَانَ عَفُوًّا غَفُورًا ۝

IV *Surah Al-Nisaa'*, **The Generous Qur'an** 4:43

****

Shaytan's plan is to stir up hatred and enmity among people by luring them to consume intoxicants and get involved in gambling. When a person takes intoxicants he will be in a state of limbo in which he may lose control over his body and decrease his self-discipline. The result is that it becomes easier for *Shaytan* to engulf him and put him on a destructive path where he will practice the prohibitted such as commission of adultery, murder or other crimes. **ALLAH** (*subhanahu wa ta'ala*) therefore did not only prohibit adultery but the path which leads to adultery as well as the

193

apparatus lying on that path, such as the liquor store. Even those who give out licences to people to sell liquor publicly are inciting man to the path of adultery or other crimes. There is therefore a chain-like contextual apparatus that leads from one evil to another which is designed to incite man and lure him to be preoccupied with illusions and deviation.[20]

****

SURAH XVII (17) *The Night Journey*

32.   And come not near unto adultery. Lo! it is an abomination and an evil way.

وَلَا تَقْرَبُوا الزِّنَى إِنَّهُ كَانَ فَاحِشَةً وَسَاءَ سَبِيلًا

XVII *Surah Al-Israa'*, **The Generous Qur'an** 17:32

****

194

****

<u>SURAH XIX (19)</u> *Mary*

59. Now there hath succeeded them a later generation who have ruined worship and have followed lusts. But they will meet deception.

نَخَلَفَ مِنْ بَعْدِهِمْ خَلْفٌ أَضَاعُوا الصَّلَوٰةَ وَاتَّبَعُوا الشَّهَوٰتِ فَسَوْفَ يَلْقَوْنَ غَيًّا

XIX *Surah Maryam*, **The Generous Qur'an** 19:59

****

Those who want to be in the path of deviation will forget *salaat* and will follow only their desires and lusts. The public realm should not allow itself to be the forum for the broadcast of lust and pornography, or the establishment of bars, gay bath-houses etc., for these are the links in the deviant *Shaytanic* chain which lead to deception, destitution and self-destruction.

195

اِنَّ اللهَ مَعَنَا   اِنَّ اللهَ مَعَنَا   اِنَّ اللهَ مَعَنَا

****

SURAH XXIV (24) *Light*

21. O ye who believe! Follow not the footsteps of the devil. Unto whomsoever followeth the footsteps of the devil, lo! he commandeth filthiness and wrong. Had it not been for the grace of Allah and His mercy unto you, not one of you would ever have grown pure. But Allah causeth whom He will to grow. And Allah is Hearer, Knower.

يَا أَيُّهَا الَّذِينَ آمَنُوا لَا تَتَّبِعُوا خُطُوَاتِ الشَّيْطَانِ وَمَن يَتَّبِعْ خُطُوَاتِ الشَّيْطَانِ فَإِنَّهُ يَأْمُرُ بِالْفَحْشَاءِ وَالْمُنكَرِ وَلَوْلَا فَضْلُ اللَّهِ عَلَيْكُمْ وَرَحْمَتُهُ مَا زَكَى مِنكُم مِّنْ أَحَدٍ أَبَدًا وَلَكِنَّ اللَّهَ يُزَكِّي مَن يَشَاءُ وَاللَّهُ سَمِيعٌ عَلِيمٌ ٢١

XXIV *Surah Al-Nur*, **The Generous Qur'an** 24:21

****

Salaat: The Medium of Purification and Remembrance

There is no way that a person who is engulfed by *Shaytan's* way would continue to practice *salaat* in the proper contextual manifestation. A person might still do *salaat* and not yet have purified himself. But *salaat* is the medium through which the process of purification has to take place. There is a process of metamorphosis from deviation to straightness, from adultery to holiness, from sickness to healthiness and from *Shaytan's* way to

196

ALLAH's (*subhanahu wa ta'ala*) Way. If a person, however, does *salaat* but continues to practice prohibitted, shameful and degrading things, he has not done the *salaat* properly. In some cases, his *salaat* is rejected.

It is known that *salaat* is meant to burn *Shaytan's* way and to establish **ALLAH's** (*subhanahu wa ta'ala*) Way constantly. By practicing **ALLAH's** (*subhanahu wa ta'ala*) Way constantly, including the physical observance of the five prayers and practicing the straightness of **ALLAH's** (*subhanahu wa ta'ala*) Way in between the prayers as one's *modus operandi* and *modus vivendi*, *Shaytanic* ways cannot establish themselves as a pattern of behavior and will never acquire legitimacy. Sickness is thereby dissolved from its roots. The idea of praying five times a day is merely the prelude for becoming conscious of praying full-time. It is also an excersize of gradual rectification.[21] The norm of praying five times a day is no more than an imperative disciplinary procedure which will burn and uproot *Shaytanic* ways when one remembers **ALLAH** (*subhanahu wa ta'ala*). This is because the name of **ALLAH** (*subhanahu wa ta'ala*) in itself, *pari passu* the Word of **ALLAH** (*subhanahu wa ta'ala*) is sovereign, supreme and absolute. No other way could establish itself when one remembers the Word of **ALLAH** (*subhanahu wa ta'ala*). **ALLAH** (*subhanahu wa ta'ala*) governs the inward and outward manifestation of his slaves. When a person starts to perform *salaat* he has to begin by reading some *Surahs* from the **Generous Qur'an**. When he reads the **Generous Qur'an** with a healthy heart and proper breath, **ALLAH** (*subhanahu wa ta'ala*) will put a veil between him and those who don't believe in the Hereafter.

197

****

SURAH XVII (17) *The Night Journey*

45.   And when thou recitest the
Qur'an We place between thee and
those who believe not in the Hereafter
a hidden barrier;

46.   And We place upon their hearts
veils lest they should understand it,
and in their ears a deafness; and when
thou makest mention of they Lord
alone in the Qur'an, they turn their
backs in aversion.

وَإِذَا قَرَأْتَ الْقُرْآنَ جَعَلْنَا بَيْنَكَ وَبَيْنَ الَّذِينَ
لَا يُؤْمِنُونَ بِالْآخِرَةِ حِجَابًا مَّسْتُورًا ۝
وَجَعَلْنَا عَلَى قُلُوبِهِمْ أَكِنَّةً أَن يَفْقَهُوهُ وَفِي
آذَانِهِمْ وَقْرًا وَإِذَا ذَكَرْتَ رَبَّكَ فِي الْقُرْآنِ وَحْدَهُ
وَلَّوْا عَلَى أَدْبَارِهِمْ نُفُورًا ۝

XVII *Surah Al-Israa'*, **The Generous Qur'an** 17:45-46
These Verses on Page 282.

****

Salaat in Islam was ordained to be performed periodically
throughout the day. There are five periods a day during which the
salaat is to be performed. These are: first, after dawn and before
sunrise, next at midday, then half-way between midday and sunset,
then after sunset, and lastly, at night after the total disappearance of
twilight.22 This makes a person to be occupied with *salaat* almost
all day, meaning that he is conscious of the contextual framework of

198

salaat . Even when one is not performing the physical aspect of *salaat* he is still "ironing" himself out straight in the private and public realm, because the same **ALLAH** (*subhanahu wa ta'ala*) to Whom he prays during the *salaat* is observing him throughout the entire day.

Islam does not have the dualism of the self-styled Christians and Jews, who go to their respective churches and temples to receive their weekly anti-dote for an hour, which preaches "thou shall not kill", only to then go into public civil society and pursue the total opposite which is the war of all against all. The self-styled Christians and self-styled Jews do not take the teaching of their *salaat* to civil society. Yet in authentic Islam, a Muslim is practicing *salaat* in his private and public realm, in his business or other activities. A true Muslim, therefore, cannot lie when he is buying and selling. He cannot forget **ALLAH** (*subhanahu wa ta'ala*) in his commerce. Nothing preoccupies him except his adherence to the Straight Way of **ALLAH** (*subhanahu wa ta'ala*). His living, or *modus operandi*, is the *praxis* of Islam itself. He remembers that **ALLAH** (*subhanahu wa ta'ala*) is observing him. The only way that he can escape **ALLAH** (*subhanahu wa ta'ala*) is to surrender to Him, which means to adhere to His laws and Ways in every segment of one's private and public life. Remembering **ALLAH** (*subhanahu wa ta'ala*) and performing *salaat* will result in cleansing him and "ironing" him inwardly because it teaches him how to live according to the Law of **ALLAH** (*subhanahu wa ta'ala*), which is the chariot of the body and soul.[23]

The dynamic and mysterious aspect of the *salaat* is that one must wash himself physically and outwardly with water prior to performing it. This is called ablution (*wudu*). After he performs

199

the *salaat* for a period of time, the *salaat* starts to wash an individual inwardly. Therefore, the *salaat* becomes a preventive force which keeps him away from deviation and shameful and unjust deeds like adultery, alcoholism and theft, etc. If one is committed to following the Path, **ALLAH** (*subhanahu wa ta'ala*) will provide sweet water, richness and happiness in abundance, beyond what the human eye ever saw or the human ear ever heard, or any human faculty could encompass.

In order for a person to read the **Generous Qur'an** and see guidance in it, there are six requisites. Believing in the Unseen is the first requisite. Then one must do the *salaat*. The third requisite is to give out of what **ALLAH** (*subhanahu wa ta'ala*) has provided. The fourth is to believe in what **ALLAH** (*subhanahu wa ta'ala*) revealed to the **Prophet Muhammad** (*prayers and peace of **ALLAH** be upon him*) *in toto,* and to believe in what **ALLAH** (*subhanahu wa ta'ala*) revealed prior to his appearance on earth. Finally, one should be certain of the Hereafter. After fulfilling these requirements expressed in *Surah Baqara, Ayat* 1-5, a person could find guidance in the **Generous Qur'an**. He will reap the fruits of a successful harvest.

Obtaining the station of being from the *muttaqeen* (those having piety) is not a simple task. Obtaining a Ph.D. or a billion dollars, by comparison, would be trivial to this task. They are incommensurable goals at that. But first, one has to be called, and **ALLAH** (*subhanahu wa ta'ala*) guides whomever He wants.

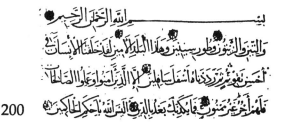

200

The Generous Qur'an as the Only Authentic Book

It is imperative to know that any books ever known to humankind other than the **Generous Qur'an** are short-lived. In other words, through the march of history, man has glorified and, to a certain extent, worshipped the human intellect. Many people write books. Some books are only contemporaneously relevant to the local space dimension and local time dimension. Some books which are written about certain concepts extracted from the **Generous Qur'an** have transcended their time dimension and locality in their relevance and applicability. However, none of them have ever proclaimed that they are a substitute for the **Generous Qur'an** and/or that they encompass what the **Generous Qur'an** encompasses. Therefore, no single one of these books ever proclaimed to be the total aggregation of reality. The main common denominator that one finds among the authentic Muslim authors of books about Islam and the **Generous Qur'an** is that they asserted their human limitations in the face of the fact that **A L L A H** (*subhanahu wa ta'ala*) knows best.

It is imperative to know that there is no one book other than the **Generous Qur'an** which is complete, without any kind of crookedness or flaw either in its linguistic articulation or profound eloquence, in its empirical or conceptual meaning, in its contemporaneous and historical applicability, etc., and in its congruity and perfection between thought and *praxis*. The **Generous Qur'an** is the only book which has survived throughout all history without having been altered, changed or modified. It is the only book which is continuously applicable in its totality without a gap between theory and *praxis*. It is the only book which

201

delineates the normal trajectory of the *modus operandi* and *modus vivendi* of the indeterminant human estate throughout the spaceship earth.[24] It is the only authentic, divinely-ordained, holistic, holy and sacred book that has been kept in its total autonomy since it was revealed. In simple terms, it is the only book that gives sane, normal and straight solutions for any human being, regardless of his geographical location. This is true whether the human being is in the *kufur* east or *kufur* west, whether he is in the *kufur* north or *kufur* south.

At this level of consciousness, it is imperative that any individual ask **ALLAH** (*subhanahu wa ta'ala*) for guidance. If **ALLAH** (*subhanahu wa ta'ala*) does not give Light to an individual or to a civilization, that individual or civilization will never have Light. The first step towards guidance is that the person makes total surrender to the Lord, and declares his *Din*, his way, to be Islam. Thereby, he can become the embodiment of *Shari'atu* **ALLAH** (*subhanahu wa ta'ala*). The *Shari'ah* is the abiding force of history, because **ALLAH** (*subhanahu wa ta'ala*) will forgive any transgression except that others are worshipped beside Him. Creation is the domain of **ALLAH** (*subhanahu wa ta'ala*), and we are His slaves. To know what this means, a person has to read the **Generous Qur'an** in Arabic and to practice the *Din* of **ALLAH** (*subhanahu wa ta'ala*). Thereby, the Light, the jewels and the pearls will reveal themselves. Whatever your Lord *is*, you are *his*. And this is just the beginning.

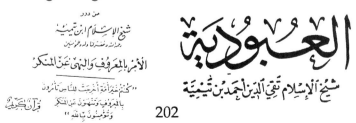

202

Endnotes

[1]Charles Wendell (translator), *Five Tracts of Hasan Al-Banna'*, (Berkeley, California: University of California Press, 1978), pp. 42-99.

[2]Sheikh Muzaffer Ozak Al-Jerrahi, *The Unveiling of Love: Sufism and the Remembrance of God*, (New York: Inner Traditions International, 1981), pp. 23-56.

[3]Ibid., pp. 79-127.

[4]Sheikh Fadhlalla Haeri, *Journey of the Universe as Expounded in the Qur'an*, (London; Boston: KPI, 1985), pp. 42-79.

[5]Sabih Ahmad Kamali (translator), *Al-Ghazali's Tahafut Al-Falasifah [Incoherence of the Philosophers]*, (Lahore, Pakistan: Pakistan Philosophical Congress, 1963), pp. 13-53.

[6]Sheikh Muzaffer Ozak Al-Jerrahi, Op. Cit.

[7]Mohamed Ahmed Sherif, *Ghazali's Theory of Virtue*, (Albany, New York: State University of New York Press, 1975), pp. 77-104.

[8]Muhammad Abul Quasem, *Salvation of the Soul and Islamic Devotions*, (London: Kegan Paul International; 1983), pp. 85-176.

[9]Faqir Nur Muhammad Sarwari Qadri, *Irfan: A True and Unique Book of Divine Knowledge,* (Lahore, Pakistan: Ripon Printing Press. n.d.), pp. 39-67.

[10]Sheikh Muzaffer Ozak Al-Jerrahi, Op. Cit.

[11]Taqee Ad-Deen Ibn Taymiyah, *Al-'Uboodiyah: The Essay of Worship,* (Elizabeth, New Jersey: Daar Al-Hadeeth, 1987), pp. 19-56.

[12]Muhammad Al-Ghazzali, *Our Beginning in Wisdom,* (New York: Octagon Books, 1975), pp. 1-45.

[13]Charles Wendell, Op. Cit., pp. 21-57.

[14]Sheikh Muzaffer Ozak Al-Jerrahi, Op. Cit., pp. 77-103.

[15]Faqir Nur Muhammad Sarwari Qadri, Op. Cit., pp. 105-172.

[16]Muhammad Abul Quasem, Op. Cit.

[17]B. A. Dar, "Ethical Teachings of the Qur'an", in M. M. Sharif (editor), *A History of Muslim Philosophy*, (Wiesbaden, Germany: Otto Harrassowitz, 1963), pp. 155-177.

[18]Ibid.

[19]Muhammad Abul Quasem, Op. Cit.

[20]Charles Wendell, Op. Cit., pp. 42-99.

[21]Sheikh Muzaffer Ozak Al-Jerrahi, Op. Cit., pp. 104-136.

[22]Muhammad Abul Quasem, Op. Cit.

[23]Sheikh Muzaffer Ozak Al-Jerrahi, Op. Cit.

[24]Sheikh Fadhlalla Haeri, Op. Cit., 1-40.

205

APPENDIX

Other Publications and Manuscripts by the Authors

1969. *The Function of the Military Base in the Nuclear Age*, Master's Thesis, Eastern Connecticut State College, by Hassan El-Yacoubi.

1973. *The Evolution of Palestinian Consciousness*, Ph.D. Dissertation, University of Colorado at Boulder, by Dr. Hassan El-Yacoubi.

1974. *Political Economy and the Backward Motion of History*, by Dr. Hassan El-Yacoubi.

1974. *The American and Palestinian Humanistic Synthesis*, by Dr. Hassan El-Yacoubi.

1975. "Scientific Technology and General System Theory as Applied to Public Administration", by Dr. Hassan El-Yacoubi. Appearing in *African Administrative Studies*, (No. 13, January, 1975, pp. 91-101).

1975. *The Relevance of Alexis de Tocqueville to Contemporary Technocratic Democracy*, Master's Thesis, University of Colorado at Boulder, by "Amar" Jane El-Yacoubi.

1976. *In Search of a Theory: The Episteme of Knowledge and the Disappearance of Man*, by Dr. Hassan El-Yacoubi.

1976. **"System Analysis, System Management, and Scientific Typology as Applied to Development in the Third World"**, by Dr. Hassan El-Yacoubi. Appearing in *Impact of Science on Society*, (UNESCO, Vol. 26, No. 3, May-September, 1976). This article appeared in five languages.

1976. *Al-Natharat Al-Sabi'* (Seven Perspectives), by Sheikh Salime Abu Al-Iqbal Hassan Filasteen El-Yacoubi, *Mufti Jaffa* (Governor of Jaffa, Palestine). In Arabic.

1977. *Science and the Entropy of Civilization, Vol. I: The Fragile Foundation of Contemporary Science*, by Dr. Hassan El-Yacoubi.

1977-78. *Science, Technology, Administration and Development: Perspectivism, Vol. I & II,* by Dr. Hassan El-Yacoubi and "Amar" Jane El-Yacoubi.

إِنَّ اللَّهَ مَعَنَا

The Arabic, Qur'anic and Islamic Paradigm:
Light, Jewels and Pearls

وَمَا تَوْفِيقِي إِلَّا بِاللَّهِ عَلَيْهِ تَوَكَّلْتُ وَإِلَيْهِ أُنِيبُ

1979. *Science and the Entropy of Civilization, Vol. II,* by Dr. Hassan El-Yacoubi and "Amar" Jane El-Yacoubi.

1983. *A Comparative Analysis of Islamic and Western Democratic Thought*, Ph.D. Dissertation, University of Colorado at Boulder, by Dr. "Amar" Jane El-Yacoubi.

1983. *The Cyclical Pattern of the American Presidential-Congressional Interplay*, by Dr. Hassan El-Yacoubi and Dr. "Amar" Jane El-Yacoubi.

1983. *Comparative Political Economy: A Developmental Analysis*, by Dr. Hassan El-Yacoubi and Dr. "Amar" Jane El-Yacoubi.

Persons interested in corresponding with the authors, or in obtaining a copy of any of the above materials, should write to the following address:

Drs. H. & J. El-Yacoubi
P.O. Box 4094
Boulder, Colorado
80306 U.S.A.

208

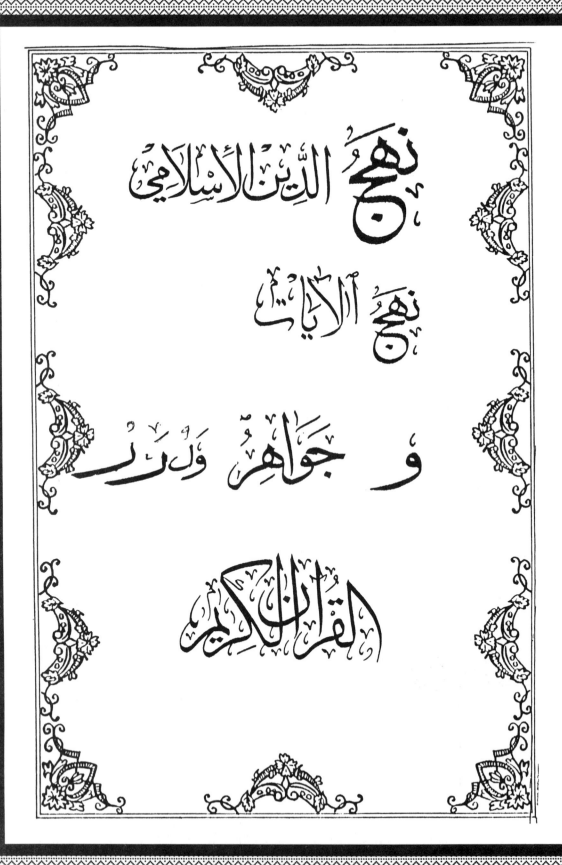

نهج الدين الإسلامي

نهج الآيات

و جواهر وكنز

القرآن الكريم